The Perfect Pistol Shot

This book is dedicated to my first firearm instructor, my dad.

The Perfect Pistol Shot

Albert H. League III

Paladin Press • Boulder, Colorado

The Perfect Pistol Shot
by Albert H. League III

Copyright © 2011 by Albert H. League III

ISBN 13: 978-1-161004-571-1
Printed in the United States of America

Published by Paladin Press, a division of
Paladin Enterprises, Inc.
Gunbarrel Tech Center
7077 Winchester Circle
Boulder, Colorado 80301 USA
+1.303.443.7250

Direct inquiries and/or orders to the above address.

Front cover photo © iStockphoto.com/Chris Hutchison

Visit our website at www.paladin-press.com

CONTENTS

ACKNOWLEDGMENTS

I would like to acknowledge the assistance of, and thank in no particular order, the Cigar Fellowship, Cpl. and Mrs. Perry, 1st Sgt. and Mrs. Ganiszewski, Instructor Rod Trumpf, Master Shooter Aaron Gibson and the FTU at Vancouver PD, Buzz and Mrs. Horch, the Professor and the Iron Man, Mr. Peckerwood, Aileen and the Barker boys, Jack League, Sheriff and Mrs. Mitchell, the good folks at Wackenhut Services Inc. for their interest in firearm safety, Donna DuVall and Jon Ford of Paladin Press, and finally, that green gun club, wherein the priests of marksmanship work their magic—the United States Marine Corps.

INTRODUCTION

☆☆☆☆☆

A CASE FOR

MARKSMANSHIP TRAINING

King Solomon taught, "There is nothing new under the sun."
He must have been a fine handgun instructor. Knowledge of
what it takes to strike a target with a handheld firearm has not dramatically increased over the last two centuries. Lasers and multistage
triggers did not change the Fundamentals of Marksmanship, they val-
idated them. The experienced shooter may question whether a book
on the Fundamentals of Marksmanship is worth reading. After all,
even novice shooters understand how to align sights, squeeze the
trigger, and avoid unnecessary movement while shooting. It is also
true that high school driver education classes teach steering, braking,
passing, and turning, which are exactly the skills needed to be a Formula One driver. Passing driver's ed class will not make you a race
car driver, and stumbling through the Fundamentals of Marksmanship will not make you a great shot.

This book does not suggest new ideas nor advocate recent trends.
This book is an attempt to make the case for something very old—
the fundamental principles of marksmanship. It is the intensity, the
degree, by which a shooter applies the Fundamentals of Marksmanship that enables the perfect shot. More importantly, a full understanding of these principles enables the shooter to self-correct while
shooting, avoid panic, and overcome shooting obstacles such as sub-

stituted firearms, poor lighting, psychological duress, lack of practice, and distance.

If you wish to understand firearm marksmanship, consider the typewriter. The typewriter is a tool, a mechanical device that allows the user to utilize the machine by manipulating controls to produce predetermined and consistent results. The same is true for operating a pistol. I doubt anyone believes his typewriter has existential properties; certainly no one considers the successful typist a possessor of supernatural and intuitive powers. Yet, in the field of marksmanship there is a strong undercurrent of, well, mysticism. Both the handgun and its user are often dunked in romantic notions that no one would ever ascribe to the typist. That's unfair, because the typist requires the greater physical skill and the typewriter is a far more complex machine than any firearm.

The difference in treatment is entirely emotional; the firearm, wrapped in mystery to most of the world, followed the sword. The commonplace typewriter followed the pen. Moreover, there is the matter of training. When the typewriter entered the workplace a century ago, training began by the numbers, exactingly and repetitively manipulating the device to achieve particular results—press the "T" key and the letter "T" appears on the paper.

Marksmanship came out of antiquity laden with unfortunate assumptions. Possibly having roots in crossbow shooting, firearm marksmanship was being discovered before sights were affixed to muskets. That slow, disjointed roll forward has gathered a lot of superstition detrimental to good shooting. Even worse, unlike typing, where perfection is demanded, successful shooting is rarely held to an objective standard based on conditions and mechanical capacity. If you doubt that claim, visit a local police range, where "qualified" often means eight times less accurate than mechanical accuracy can produce. Accept that standard in typing and "Dear Sir" becomes "Solj Dcg."

Firearms are tools for hunting, sporting devices, and implements of recreation, but above all else, firearms are weapons. That martial truth has caused great mischief in shooter learning. The word "combat" is a fashionable descriptor overused in handgun literature. It implies a trade knowledge or secret understanding of the "real way" to shoot a firearm. That thinking is why at least one California sheriff's academy in the 1980s had cadets place duct tape over pistol sights. ("In combat you'll never use the sights.") That produced peace officers who could not reliably hit a dinner plate at 15 yards.

Simply standing on a firing line practicing marksmanship, combat experts tell us, will never translate to useable combat skills. Bet me: there is no basis on which to build tactical firearm skills *other* than marksmanship.

Close-range encounters (5 yards or less) account for the majority of actual police shootings. From this, combat trainers incorrectly conclude that point shooting techniques (called by a new name every week) must be the basis for defensive shooting programs. A myth has arisen in firearm literature that claims rigid bull's-eye training dominates law enforcement, against which a few informed instructors are advocating "combat shooting." It's just not true. During the last 30 years, most law enforcement academies have deemphasized marksmanship in favor of combat shooting. Unfortunately, most police officers involved in close-range shootings miss their targets despite the trend toward "realistic" training. As distance increases to a car length or so, it only gets worse.

Before I go further, let me clarify my position for the reader—good tactical skills and techniques are essential for the defensive shooter. This is not an "either/or" proposition. But whether you want to shoot squirrels, punch holes in paper targets, or defend your home, you must master the Fundamentals of Marksmanship on which you may build tactical skills.

Imagine your eight-year-old son tells you he wants to grow up to be a professional quarterback. You could take him into the backyard and teach him how to hold a football. Then you might stand a few yards apart and throw the ball back and forth. Of course, that is not "realistic situational training," which requires four or five 300-pound men to chase junior around mom's perennial planter while he tries to find an open receiver. That probably would not be productive training. If you want to box, first learn where to put your feet. If you want to be a brain surgeon, start by handling a dead frog. If you want to shoot accurately and quickly, start by mastering the sights.

Training works. For good or for ill, you can be trained to act under duress. In 1970, near Newhall, California, four California Highway Patrol officers were killed in a shooting involving two suspects. One of the fallen officers was found in possession of expended brass from his revolver. It is largely accepted that the officer placed the brass in his pocket as a result of a CHP range practice that prohibited shooters from dropping expended brass onto the range. The CHP officer was therefore "trained" to use fine motor skills to collect empty cartridges expelled from his revolver even under the severe stress of an armed attack.

Physical and emotional duress diminishes a shooter's abilities, without question. This makes perfect training all the more important. If a shooter can't hit his mark under perfect conditions, he can't do it under life-threatening conditions. Training and practice must be deliberate.

Speed is valuable to almost all shooters regardless of particular interest. If you want to shoot accurately more quickly, first train to shoot accurately. Then practice perfectly and you'll become a quicker shot. If you own a house key, you've already proven this principle. You can probably unlock your front door in the dark and enter your home within three seconds. You take out your key as you approach, slip it into the lock, and turn it far enough to retract the bolt. Before the key is released, you cross the threshold. You achieved this competence not by practicing key speed every weekend but through repetitive and proper use of the key.

Again, I am not advocating doing away with timed shooting drills, but such exercises are for improvement of existing skills, not their establishment. Shooting under such simulated stress as time limits, physical exercise, and reduced lighting are mandatory elements of a tactical training program. Such training complements but does not replace the formal teaching of marksmanship. Knowing how to "engage" targets is valuable for the defensive shooter, but if "engage" doesn't translate into "hit," what is the point?

In general, most shooters don't know why they hit or why they miss, and most trainers are simply gun enthusiasts who act as safety officers. Many competent peace officers go to the qualification range each year not knowing whether they'll qualify. The private sector is no better. I witnessed a young woman in Portland, Oregon, pay a private range instructor 50 bucks an hour to teach her to shoot foot-and-a-half groups at 5 yards. She would have done better throwing rocks. Marksmanship is science, not art. Every time a shooter takes a deliberate action, a particular result will occur. There is no mystery to good shooting, only ignorance of the Fundamentals of Marksmanship. My intention for this book is to make mastery of marksmanship, the perfect shot, attainable to the average shooter.

Originally, I had titled this book *That Ancient Magic: The Perfect Pistol Shot*. The good people at Paladin Press wisely changed the title to save me from being shelved with *The Junior Magician's Guide to Card Tricks* and *Pull a Rabbit out of Your Hat!* Since I am opposed to the mystification of shooting, the intended name of this book may have brought some charges of hypocrisy. Admittedly, *That Ancient Magic* does seem at odds with the philosophy of this book. But on a crisp autumn day, when the woods are quiet and the sun is just starting to drop, take a good revolver for a walk and bring your will to bear at 20 or 30 paces. I think you'll have to admit, the whole thing is just a little bit magic.

Good shooting,
A. H. League III

☆☆☆☆☆

GETTING THE MOST
FROM THIS BOOK

The information provided in this book is derived from my Fundamentals of Marksmanship class. The lecture that always precedes my range training is the substance of this book. It has been my experience of many years that firearm training must begin academically. At the core of what a student needs to shoot well is not purely technical knowledge. It is not a question of putting your feet so many inches apart or leaning forward a few degrees. What the student needs to know first is "why" and then "what."

When the Fundamentals of Marksmanship are understood, the shooter will know where to put his feet and how to maneuver his body within whatever shooting environment he finds himself. It does little good to memorize stances, grips, and other techniques that may not always be possible due to physical environment and immediate circumstances (lying on the ground, diminished physical capacity, straddling a wall, etc.). To be sure, there is proper grip and proper stance and certainly proper trigger control, but the goal of this book is to persuade, educate, and challenge the reader to gain *experiential* knowledge that will enable self-coaching of every shot.

Hopefully, this book is written in such a way as to bring the reader along the path to mastery of marksmanship. Chapter 1 is a practical safety refresher. Chapters 2 through 5 cover the Fundamentals of Marksmanship, which is the philosophy behind the practice and must be understood for the reader to benefit from this book. Chapter 6 discusses the practical application of the Fundamentals, putting them together for successful shooting. Chapter 7 instructs the reader on fixing shooting problems and self-coaching. The last chapter is intended to help the reader be a discerning and successful member of the shooting community.

There have been countless books and videos on "how to shoot." They all involve the same gray and black sight alignment diagram, the obligatory modified Weaver stance displays, and of course some good illustrations of "proper grip." All that may be quite worthwhile. Yet despite the popularity of such material over the last 50 years, the shooting public cannot shoot accurately. Marksmanship must be learned academically because it is an intellectual pursuit. Therefore, I have sincerely tried not to write yet another imitate-the-pictures guide to handgun shooting. You would not try to fly a jet simply by mimicking pilots you had observed; don't try it with marksmanship. There is no gimmick or shortcut to becoming a better shot—either you understand the Fundamentals of Marksmanship or you do not. There is nothing in between.

USING THIS BOOK

1. Read it thoroughly, cover to cover, while noting everything with which you disagree. (Mark it up—neither author nor publisher will be angry if you have to buy a second copy.)
2. Complete each "Prove It" exercise as you encounter them in the book.
3. When you finish the book, review your notes and decide whether you still disagree.
4. Reread the first seven chapters of this book (it is not *War and Peace*).

5. Realize that if you want to shoot better than you do, you will have to shoot differently. Consider what changes the book requires you to make.
6. Decide to trust or test the material in this book by fanatically executing the Fundamentals of Marksmanship.
7. Use a mirror to check your posture and natural point of aim as described in this book.
8. Find a safe place to dry fire using the techniques in this book. Use proper sighting to control the dry fire sequence.
9. Go to the range and train as outlined in the training chapter of this book.
10. Check your results against the objective standard given at the end of this section.

Most of what I have put into this book was gained while serving in the United States Marine Corps. The Marines have understood and taught marksmanship for two centuries. I certainly received valuable firearm training during my law enforcement career, from several instructors, though I found no better method of hitting a target than the discipline of traditional marksmanship. The principles laid out in this book, as previously stated, are not new, nor did they originate with me. Writers like Col. Jeff Cooper and Elmer Keith were advocating the study of marksmanship long before I ever saw a handgun. The best I can hope for is to supply the student with the argument for marksmanship, clearly teach the fundamentals, and offer a few persuasive exercises with the intention of converting the shooter from an imitator of others into a thinking marksman.

MARKSMANSHIP AND BELIEF

In teaching marksmanship, persuasion is the challenge. The student who does not believe will not try. One of the great advantages to teaching marksmanship to women is they have no social ax to grind—the instructor has expertise, the student wants to learn, and the transfer of knowledge is easy. On the other hand, every man in this country is an expert on firearms. Men who have never held a firearm already have preferences and expectations. Any fellow who has shot more than five rounds is ready to teach.

Marksmanship *as a study* is a hard sell for the instructor. Overall, I've done rather well convincing shooters to trust the information. Of course, some have been easier than others. I have only a single recollection of utterly failing to persuade a student. A county correctional officer could not qualify with her service weapon. She came to remedial training and was not responding. We alternated instructors, tried various drills, asked questions, and generally attempted to coax her into learning. Eventually, she dropped the pretense and made it clear that she considered the whole matter to be foolishness taught by idiots. There was no reason for that shooter not to be able to shoot well—no reason other than unwillingness to trust the material. Her hands and eyes were quite capable of shooting perfect shots; her mind was not. Marksmanship is an intellectual pursuit. It must be understood and then physically applied.

Throughout this book you will find "Prove It" exercises designed to allow you to test the concepts offered without the stress of actual shooting. I encourage you to complete the exercises rather than simply reading them. You are far more apt to trust the memory of experience than to recall something you saw or read.

A VERIFIABLE STANDARD FOR MEASURING THIS BOOK

The material in this book has been successfully taught to U.S. Marines, Japanese security personnel, deputies sheriff, police officers, correctional officers, federal contract security personnel, and private citizens. Shooters (with no physical impairment and a safe, modern, full-size handgun of centerfire caliber) properly applying the information in this book should expect *no less than*:

Three shots in one ragged hole at 7 yards

Three shots *within* 4 inches at 25 yards

Consistent torso hits on a full-size silhouette
at 100 yards

It is impossible to convert the information in this book to knowledge and not shoot well. I welcome the reader to use the above standard in measuring the value of the information provided and in judging my competence as an instructor.

CHAPTER ONE

SAFETY (MIND)

This book provides instruction in marksmanship and is not a "first time" shooter's guide. Before mastering the Fundamentals of Marksmanship, *it is incumbent upon the reader to receive professional instruction in the safe operation of his firearm.* Safety is the foundation of good firearms handling and therefore worthy of mention. There are two subjects in firearm instruction that are typically undertaught. The first is shotgun training (the redheaded stepchild of law enforcement firearm instruction) and the second is safety. If you experienced a formal introduction to shooting (military service, police academy, hunter safety training, etc.), you received safety training. Afterward, you very likely only received a cursory review of safety rules.

Every shooter of some experience has encountered unintentional discharges of a firearm. Some that I'm aware of include a shotgun blast through the roof of a SWAT van, one round into the buttocks of a police officer while inside the department locker room, two rounds fired while unloading a revolver (still inexplicable), and a shot to the ballistic vest during a security guard quick-draw contest. Safety violations go beyond shots fired; a staggering number of shooters cannot chamber a round into their pistols without endangering those around them. Time spent in acquiring firearm safety skills is never wasted.

FAMILIARITY BREEDS CONTEMPT

Handgun safety has two enemies: ignorance and habit. Years ago, I attended a class for law enforcement firearm instructors. One of my fellow students was a remarkable shooter from a large, metro SWAT team. This officer was very active in state-level speed shooting competitions. To understand this officer's actions, it's helpful to know that law enforcement ranges are typically "hot"—officers are expected to always have a loaded weapon, even off the firing line. This practice trains officers to never let their weapons remain unloaded in the field. Civilian sport shooting events are typically "cold" ranges, where shooters are not allowed to have loaded weapons off the firing line. When our SWAT officer stepped off the firing line, he engaged another student in conversation about pistols. The SWAT officer pulled his pistol from the holster and showed it to the other student. The other student wisely declined to touch the weapon and the SWAT officer placed it back into his holster. Then, as was his *habit* in sport shooting on a cold range, he squeezed his trigger to drop the internal hammer and release tension. The man shot himself in the calf. This shooter was not ignorant; he was overconfident and drunk with the sloppiness of unconscious habit.

SYMPATHETIC MUSCLE REACTIONS

Guns do not "go off" by themselves any more than piles of lumber "accidentally" build a house. Having investigated an embarrassing number of unintentional shootings, I am amazed at the number of people who refuse to concentrate when manipulating a handgun. Unintentional discharges are easily avoided by keeping one's finger off the trigger until ready to shoot. Here's the problem—handguns are ergonomically designed for the human hand in the firing position. The index finger of the shooting hand naturally rests on the trigger. Lifting the finger off the trigger, even outside the trigger guard, isn't enough to avoid unintentional discharges.

When I attended the police academy, one of my instructors was a medically retired New Jersey SWAT officer whose career had ended when a fellow team member shot him from behind. Those incidents were fairly common in SWAT because team members move in tight columns. Such shootings most often occurred when an officer would slip on a rug or other obstruction. As the officer hit the ground, his muscles would tighten and his trigger finger would close on the trigger in a sympathetic reflex. You've experienced a sympathetic muscle reaction when slamming on the brakes to avoid hitting a car you were following too closely; the muscles in the neck, shoulders, and hands tighten automatically. As one hand clenches the steering wheel, the other crushes the coffee cup.

INDEXING

Simply lifting your finger off the trigger will not stop unintentional discharges. The trigger finger must be extended and pressed into the receiver or frame of the weapon (not the slide or cylinder). That's "indexing." Indexing was brought forward as the answer to unintentional discharges and effectively prevents the trigger pull caused

Single-hand grip displaying proper indexing with pistol.

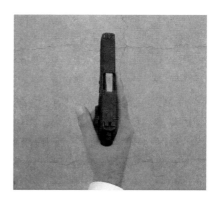

Top view of single-hand grip indexing.

Single-hand grip displaying proper indexing with revolver. (Note: Index finger avoids pressing against cylinder.)

Two-hand grip displaying proper indexing with pistol.

by a sympathetic muscle reaction. When properly indexing, a sudden occurrence that causes a sympathetic muscle reaction will only result in the trigger finger pressing harder against the frame or receiver of the weapon. Learn indexing by doing it each and every time you pick up a weapon. Protect yourself; require it of others.

Prove It: The trigger finger
will attempt to close sympathetically

For this exercise you will need 15 loose coins. Drop the coins on a tabletop. Extend your trigger finger perfectly straight. Without bending your trigger finger *even slightly*, use your other shooting-hand fingers to gather up the coins by groups of three. When you have three coins in your hand, you may drop them off to the side. Continue the process, if you can, five times until all coins have been collected. If you bend your trigger finger during the exercise, you fail.

Repeat the entire exercise with this modifica-
tion: hold out your support hand, palm up, while allowing the shooting finger to press against your
palm as you collect the coins with four shooting-
hand fingers. You will discover that by keeping the
trigger finger pressed firmly against a surface, you
may work the other fingers independently.

You cannot will your trigger finger not to have a
sympathetic muscle reaction, but you can control it
through indexing.

THE FOUR RULES OF SAFETY

There are four generally accepted rules of firearm safety. They
vary slightly from region to region but agree in substance. Known as
the "Four Rules of Safety," they are required memorization for any
competent shooter. These rules may be basic, but they are not asinine.
They can keep you out of court and prevent you from shooting a hunting buddy or being known at the local gun range as "that idiot."

#1: All guns are always loaded. Treat every weapon as if you
know it is loaded. Be willing to irritate someone who hands you a
weapon by making it completely safe, even if told, "Don't worry
about it; I already unloaded it." Making a weapon safe means the
hammer at rest on double action, external hammer weapons decocked, and the safety engaged. (These definitions are admittedly
stretched in an age when single action and double action are melding
and safeties do not always have external levers.) A safe weapon may
have rounds in the cylinder or a loaded magazine inserted.

"Completely safe" means the magazine is removed or the cylinder is emptied, the chamber is clear, the slide is locked back or the
cylinder is fully opened, and this condition has been verified by

sight and touch. Completely safe is the condition necessary to transfer physical control of the firearm in circumstances less than an emergency (there are some training and maintenance exceptions). Every year, people are shot because some idiot was certain his firearm was unloaded.

"Storage safe" is a completely safe weapon that has the cylinder closed or the slide released with the hammer decocked. In many instances, this condition is necessary to store the weapon in a small lock box or safe. This condition allows holstering.

Remember, familiarity with firearms does not guarantee safe handling. Your ex-special forces, safari hunter, SWAT-qualified brother-in-law can shoot you just as quickly as your 15-year-old, hunter-safety-class-dropout niece.

#2: Keep your finger off the trigger until ready to shoot.
Index, index, index. It takes only a fraction of a second to move the finger from frame to trigger. Readiness and speed are not lost. There is no reason for any shooter not to assume the responsibility for training his hand to automatically index. We all miss shots, we all make mistakes, and indexing converts human error from potential manslaughter to a harmless twitch against the frame of your handgun. Why wouldn't you train to acquire this skill?

#3: Never point your weapon at anything you are not willing to destroy. If the muzzle of your weapon never passes over another human being, you will never unintentionally shoot anyone. A shotgun is not a pointer, a scoped firearm is not a pair of binoculars, and a handgun is not a door knocker, prod, hammer, or magic wand. If you are not willing to destroy what is in front of your weapon, you're living dangerously. This rule does not prohibit pointing a weapon defensively, but it does require the serious evaluation of the potential threat in each case: "I will shoot if he points a gun at me" versus "I won't shoot even if he scratches my car with that key." If you aren't willing to destroy it and accept the consequences, don't point your weapon at it.

SAFETY (MIND)

An equally important component to this rule is target recognition. As a teenager I was introduced to a friend's father who was an avid hunter and shooter. That gentleman introduced me to the NRA, sponsored me at a local gun club, took me to the range, and let me shoot my first centerfire rifle. Many years later, while hunting, he shot at what he thought was a deer and inadvertently killed his nephew.

All shots are final. Confirm your target.

#4: Be aware of your backstop. You aren't just responsible for your firearm; you're also responsible for your bullets. How far do your rounds travel? Find out, because the differences in caliber and ammunition are significant. Knowing the caliber of a firearm is not sufficient to know its capabilities. In fact, ammunition may easily supersede caliber. A large-bore magnum revolver can be loaded lightly enough and a mid-caliber handgun heavy enough to reverse the ballistic pecking order. Know what is behind your target. Every round fired has consequence. A round will either strike the earth or it will strike something else, but it's not going to evaporate.

Make specific preparations for your round to stop. That means not shooting into "the woods" but shooting into "that log." Target and backstop are not always one and the same. A paper target is not a backstop. The body of a deer may be a reliable backstop for your .30-caliber rifle at some distances but not for your large-bore safari rifle. If someone is waving a gun at you and he is standing in front of 30 preschoolers, you have to make a reasoned choice whether to shoot or seek cover. Backstop considerations include (among other things) shooter skill, caliber/ammunition/bullet type/barrel length (published ballistics information), field of vision, range of hearing, proximity and movement of persons and objects, weather, type and thickness of backstop material, bullet striking angle, distance, and reason for shooting. When the round is in the weapon, the shooter is in control. *When the round leaves the muzzle, the shooter is simply an ineffectual bystander responsible for something he no longer controls.* Know your backstop.

SAFETY EQUIPMENT

Recreational shooters and, to a greater degree, law enforcement shooters are the favored prey of gimmick equipment manufacturers. I have long thought that no manufacturer ever need go out of business in this country as long as there are credulous cops. If a company makes junk baby strollers that mothers refuse to purchase, they should simply paint them black and call them "tactical range carts." However, there are two pieces of equipment worthy of investment: safety glasses and hearing protectors. Buy the best laboratory-tested equipment you can afford. Seek out reputable manufacturers with independently tested products. Glasses do more than protect against debris, and hearing protectors do more than protect the ear cavity. Educate yourself. Save your hearing and sight.

PLANNING FOR SAFETY

Safety begins with the decision to own a firearm. It is more important to choose a firearm that fits your hand rather than to choose one based on barrel length or caliber. If the handgun is too large (or too small) for the shooter's hand, it is unsafe. The pistol shooter must be able to operate the slide (and index) while keeping the pistol pointed downrange. You wouldn't buy a car if you couldn't reach the pedals or weren't strong enough to work the clutch. No modern handgun used for recreation or defense is so overwhelmingly superior to every other handgun as to be worth the compromise of a bad fit.

Storage for the firearm and ammunition should not be an afterthought—people want to steal your firearm and children want to play with them. You have an obligation to take reasonable precautions.

Safety does not occur without intention. Every shooter should seek some formal training that includes firearm safety. Read the safety manual available from your firearm manufacturer for safe handling and cleaning instructions. Join the National Rifle Association and access their excellent safety programs. In firearm safety, the best protection is a little respectful fear. Slow down, and if your mind is not on your gun handling, take a breath, relax, and pay attention. It takes a few seconds to put a weapon into a completely safe or safe condition. Spare an extra 10 seconds out of your life to save the life of another.

QUESTIONS AND ANSWERS ABOUT SAFETY

Q1: What should I do if my trigger finger doesn't quite reach the trigger with a normal grip?

A1: Trade your handgun for one that fits you. Seriously, if you cannot safely operate your weapon in the manner prescribed by the manufacturer, get another gun. Tragedy is coming for you.

Q2: I was taught that condition "safe" was sufficient to transfer a firearm. Aren't you overreaching?

A2: Almost every accidental shooting involves a false "safe." Find one case of a person shot by a handgun in completely safe mode and I'll change my mind.

Q3: I carry a revolver in a holster. Do I need to keep an empty chamber under the hammer to prevent accidental discharges?

A3: Only if your duty weapon is an old-style single-action revolver that allows the firing pin to rest on the cartridge primer. Modern, double-action revolvers are perfectly safe with a fully loaded cylinder.

Q4: Is there any danger in keeping duty pistol magazines loaded for long periods?

A4: There can be a problem. Police officers who never unload and reload their magazines risk having a round turn nose down inside the magazine, causing a failure to feed. Magazines carried on hunting and duty belts are victims of movement. Ammunition can shift even in a magazine. How long does it take to unload and reload three magazines? You can spare that much time. Also, springs fatigue under constant pressure. Save money and save your springs by rotating any extra magazines.

Q5: Should I test fire my pistol after I have cleaned it?
A5: Yes, you should. The modern service pistol is made to contend with dirt and debris. We always want a functionally clean weapon, but the amount of residue from two test rounds is absolutely nothing to a service-grade weapon. Shooters do misassemble their pistols or occasionally break them during cleaning. When would you want to find out that you made a mistake in putting your handgun back together?

Q6: Is it safer to carry duty pistols with magazines inserted but with an empty chamber?
A6: The most dangerous moment in pistol manipulation is when working the slide, and the worst time to have to chamber a round is when under severe stress. Duty pistols are considerably "safer" when safely loaded and chambered prior to duty and carried in a proper holster. This, of course, assumes a fully trained officer or home defender.

SUMMARY

Safety is much more than firearm manipulation; it is deciding what, when, and how to shoot. The entire shooting process is subordinate to safety and requires your mental presence. Do not rush yourself or others. When you don't know something, stop and call for help. Nobody wants to appear foolish, and it will probably take a couple of months for your fellow shooters to forget that you had to ask for help to unload your own weapon. That is a small price to pay to avoid committing manslaughter.

CHAPTER TWO

SIGHTING (EYES)

Sighting is to marksmanship what navigation is to air travel. Through the mastery of sighting, the shooter can know where shots will strike before they leave the weapon. Proper sighting enables the shooter to self-coach, monitor the other three Fundamentals of Marksmanship, and gain intellectual control over the entire shooting process. Sighting is always mentioned in marksmanship training but rarely sufficiently emphasized. Master sighting and you will be in the top 10 percent of the world's shooters.

Of the four Fundamentals of Marksmanship, trigger control and grip are the most difficult to learn because it requires experience of "feel" (through perfect practice). Some experts teach trigger control as the most important component of good marksmanship. They are mistaken. When you sight properly, poor trigger control can be discovered and corrected before firing. Master the trigger without mastering the sights and you will have a well-orchestrated miss. Only proper sighting has such broad impact on the entire shooting process.

Certainly, the common purpose of sights on a handgun is to align the muzzle with the target. However, mastery of the sights provides much more information. Through disciplined sighting, *every* shooting error can be seen before it occurs. For instance, when a right-handed shooter overgrips his handgun, the muzzle is turned down and to the left. The front sight travels with the muzzle, and therefore the error can be seen and corrected prior to firing.

Fortunately for an aspiring marksman, sighting is the easiest fundamental to master. In fact, after you have read this book and understand the principles of proper sighting, you will have the means to be immediately proficient. Sighting is not hard to accomplish, but rather like good driving, few perform it well.

VISUAL FOCUS

When watching a movie, you see a horse and rider in the foreground with a mountain range in the background, and all appear with equal clarity. However, in real life that's impossible. Either the horse and rider are clear and the mountain range out of focus, or the mountain range is clear and the horse and rider appear blurred. The human eye can only focus to one depth at a time. It is important to acknowledge that objects at multiple depths can be seen at once, but only one will appear clear. The blurred objects are simply out of focus but maintain shape and distance. Many shooters believe that they can keep objects at different depths in concurrent focus. In reality, those shooters are allowing their focus to flit back and forth between two or more distances. In marksmanship, that simply cannot work because *what the shooter does not see, the shooter does not control.*

Prove It: Focus is limited to one distance at a time

Extend an arm in front of you and point your thumb up. Now point your arm toward an object: wall, doorknob, tree, etc. Focus your vision on your thumb and the object beyond your thumb will appear blurry. If you change your focus to make the

object beyond your thumb clear, your thumb will
appear blurred.

You have proven that the eye cannot visually
focus at two depths at the same time.

THE TWO CHALLENGES

Sighting has two big challenges, one technical and the other
somewhat psychological. The technical dilemma in sighting is that
there are three distinct sighting points at three different depths: the
rear sight, the front sight tip, and the target. We know only one of
those can be seen clearly and the other two will appear blurred. Since
the shooter can only focus to one depth at a time, on which sighting
point should the shooter focus?

First, we have to determine the purpose of visual focus. *Visual
focus is the intelligence-gathering portion of marksmanship. It allows
control of the entire firing sequence by informing the shooter of
where the shot will go before the round has left the barrel.* With that
in mind, if we watch the target, our purpose of controlling the firing
sequence becomes unachievable because the target provides no information concerning where the weapon is pointed. (A little further on
we will discuss why the target holds the greatest temptation for
shooter focus.)

The rear sight (blurred or clear) is the closest of the three sighting points to the shooter; however, the rear sight sits atop the chambered round but is behind the point at which the bullet will leave the
control of the shooter. Therefore, the rear sight is passive and has no
active control over where the round will travel.

The front sight sits over the end of the barrel and does not devi-
ate from the muzzle; where the barrel is pointed, the front sight is
pointed. *The front sight is the device we must focus on to control the
flight path of the bullet, because it indicates the very last point at*

which the shooter can influence the bullet. I realize that the time it takes for a bullet to travel the length of a barrel is not sufficient for any sighting correction to occur. However, we can control the imperceptible amount of time when the bullet is traveling down the barrel by controlling the muzzle before and after the round is fired. The front sight tip is, for aiming purposes, the muzzle.

The rear sight, when properly out of focus, is still perfectly useable because "out of focus" will not change the shape or size of the rear sight. Using an out-of-focus rear sight to center a crystal-clear front sight will allow much more exactness than human and mechanical accuracy can ever use.

When you drive a car and properly focus on the road in front of you, blurred peripheral objects such as signs and other cars are still recognizable to you, even at speed. Likewise, the target must be blurred or the front sight will be out of focus. A bull's-eye target when out of focus is still perfectly round, with no size distortion.

The psychological challenge is that firearm sighting is unnatural and goes against the instinct of every human being who tries it. The unnatural quality of sighting is what prevents 90 percent of the shooting population from ever getting beyond mediocrity. When you throw a ball, it is natural for you to focus on the person to whom you are throwing. In fact, you could not throw a ball with any accuracy if you did not look at your target. If you focused on the ball, you would certainly miss your target. In marksmanship, the shooter must train to act unnaturally. Focus on the front sight tip and not the intended target.

One of the most common shooter errors at all levels of experience is allowing the eye to drift to the target just before the round is fired. There is always a strong natural desire to look at the target. In target shooting we want to *confirm* the target before firing. In defensive shooting the problem is often magnified when it becomes necessary to shout commands or warnings ("Drop the gun!" "Don't come any closer!" etc.). There is a natural, even logical human urge to look directly at whom we are speaking. That is why so many police officers miss their targets at remarkably close range; the mouth speaks and the eyes naturally leave the sights. So, we must act *unnaturally*, focusing intently on the front sight tip even while speaking. Remember, fanatical focus does not prevent us seeing beyond the sights; it simply prioritizes visual clarity. Understanding the principles of proper sighting, along with perfect training, are the keys to overcoming the dangerous impulse to drift visual focus from the front sight tip onto the target.

DOMINANT EYE

Just as most people are either left- or right-handed, most people have a dominant eye. Typically, though not always, the dominant eye will match the dominant hand. This matters to shooters, because the sights and target are revealed to us through perspective. If a person drives south on a California freeway, the ocean is to the driver's right. If the driver heads north, the ocean will be on his left. Neither the freeway nor the ocean change location; the driver determines position based on immediate perspective. Likewise, the shooter determines the relative position of the sights and target based on the perspective of the dominant eye.

Some shooters may need help determining their dominant eye. To do so, hold your thumb out in front of your face. Focus on your thumb while shutting one eye at a time. You will notice that when you close one of your eyes, your thumb will appear to shift a bit more than when you close the other eye. That occurs because even when trying to center an object in our vision, we tend to align based on our dominant eye.

When shooting a handgun, it is preferable to keep both eyes open. Two eyes witnessing the sights are obviously better than one eye, causing a triangulation of eyes and sights. However, the eyes are not equal and the shooter must align the sights off the dominant eye. If you truly do not have a dominant eye, use your shooting-hand eye (right hand, right eye). In rare cases where a crisscross of eye and hand occur, an adjustment can be made in body alignment (which we

will discuss later). Most likely, a shooter will naturally use the dominant eye to shoot in the same way he uses the dominant eye in view-
ing the world around him. Deliberately using your dominant eye each
time will encourage stronger sighting, consistency, and most often
better body alignment. In other words, you will shoot better.

EYE RELIEF

Another way in which perspective influences marksmanship is in
the distance between the eye and the rear sight. This is called "eye relief." The farther the rear sight is from the eye (within reason), the finer
the sights will appear and therefore the more precise sight alignment
may be achieved. Likewise, when a handgun has a longer sight radius
(distance between the two sights, usually coinciding with barrel
length), better sight alignment and sight picture will be possible. However, acquiring the sights with a long sight radius takes more time,
which may be acceptable to target shooters but unacceptable to defensive shooters (we will discuss handgun selection in another chapter).
Proper eye relief is achieved when the weapon is kept at arm's length
from the eye, which we will examine when discussing positioning of
the body. Eye relief must be consistent in all of your shooting, because
marksmanship knowledge is built upon each shot fired.

Do not lengthen eye relief by leaning backward for greater distances. Perfect your stance (and eye relief) and use it every time regardless of distance. If you know how to shoot at 15 yards, you know
how to shoot at 150 yards. It's not like throwing a football. You don't
have to shoot any "harder" for distance; the ammunition does the
work for you. When you alter eye relief, it is as if you are firing a different weapon with different sights. Consistency in sighting is consistency in bullet placement.

MECHANICAL SIGHTS

Since the subject of this chapter is handgun sighting, it would be helpful to mention the actual sighting apertures. The common front sight is a blade affixed to the muzzle end of the barrel, which will appear during sighting as a vertical bar with a clean, crisp top edge. Some will have dots or colored inserts to aid in low light or quicker sight acquisition. *Nonetheless, the tip of the front sight, for aiming purposes, is the top of the blade as seen by the shooter during aiming, not a dot or colored insert.*

The rear sight is affixed to the top of the chamber end of the handgun, in line with the barrel. The rear sight may be adjustable for windage and/or elevation or it may not. During sighting, the rear sight will appear to have a squared U shape, with two equal vertical flats standing atop either end of a horizontal plane.

A word about adjustable sights. Generally speaking, the factories do a pretty good job of setting the sights. Still, you *may* have to adjust your sights for elevation (up and down) or for windage (right and left), but do not touch the sights until you consistently fire perfect shots that perfectly group in the wrong place. Otherwise, you will, in essence, be shooting blind. Fix the shooter before ever touching the sights.

SIGHT ALIGNMENT AND SIGHT PICTURE

Let's discuss the mechanics of sighting. Sighting is broken down into two elements: sight alignment and sight picture.

Sight alignment is the positioning of the sights as viewed by the shooter. *Proper* sight alignment is the front sight blade positioned evenly on both sides as it is seen through the image of the rear sight. If light appears on either side of the front sight blade, the light should be exactly equal on both sides. The tip of the blade must appear to form a perfectly flat horizontal plane between the tops of the two vertical arms of the rear sight. The front sight tip must be crystal clear, and the rear sight must be out of focus. In other words, the front sight blade (with the crystal-clear tip) should appear to evenly fill the center of the U-shaped space that appears in the out-of-focus rear sight aperture. The sights are simply a mechanical engineer's puzzle designed to communicate to the shooter how the designer intended for the firearm to be aimed.

Sight picture is sight alignment superimposed on the target. *Proper* sight picture is a crystal-clear front sight tip perfectly positioned horizontally and vertically within an out-of-focus rear sight and held at the proper aiming point on an out-of-focus target.

POINT OF AIM

So, we align the sights properly while placing them on the point of aim. The point of aim is simply the exact point on the target at which we are aiming the weapon and, most often, where we intend for the bullet to strike. The exception is when sight alignment is deliberately held at a point other than the intended point of impact to compensate for wind or distance. For instance, a 200-meter pistol shot with nonadjustable sights would require a point of aim well above the target to allow for significant drop of the round. A target shooter may choose to hold to a higher point on the target at 50 yards than when firing at 25 yards. These are exceptions, and it must be noted that regardless of distance, wind, or nonadjustable sights, the shooter is still obliged to know his backstop and to understand where his rounds will travel.

INTENSITY

You have probably heard about sight alignment many times before reading this book, but here is the difference—*intensity*. When I say focus on the front sight tip, I mean you should see every scratch, dent, ding, and discoloration on the tip of your front sight blade. *If you can't pick your used pistol out of a group of the same make and model by the front sight alone, you aren't focusing on your front sight during shooting.*

Intensity of focus is not only necessary, it is practical. In his book *Guns, Bullets, and Gunfights*, Jim Cirillo, a veteran of multiple gun-

SIGHTING (EYES)

Typical wear and discoloration of an average service pistol front sight, providing a unique and exacting point of focus. (Note: Bluing absent from corners of front sight and thin "white line" across top of front sight makes an excellent point of focus.)

fights with the New York City PD Stakeout Unit, recalled his uncompromising front sight focus during an actual shooting when he wrote, "As I popped up from concealment to make my challenge, I experienced a miraculous phenomenon. My pistol sights came into view as clearly and precisely and steadily as if I were at one of the many pistol matches I had attended."

Perfect sighting is a matter of zealotry. Why? Because the eye must have all information concerning sight alignment and sight picture in order to ask the hand to make adjustments within hundredths of an inch. It is impossible to properly aim unless the eye is focused on the front sight tip. The body is in constant motion. The hand and therefore the handgun are *always* moving. The shooter cannot control what the shooter does not see. Casual observation is fine for determining quarters of an inch, not hundredths of an inch. This is why many shooters are unable to shoot perfectly despite hours of practice.

Reason this out for yourself: if the muzzle is pointed down, the bullet will *always* travel downward. If the muzzle is pointed to the left, the bullet will *always* travel to the left. The rules of nature will have to reverse themselves for anything else to occur. So, if we can command the exact location of the front sight tip within proper sight alignment and proper sight picture, we can control bullet placement. Some skill is required, but that's all—*some* skill. There is no mystery to good shooting; it requires only a fanaticism that is well within reach of the average shooter.

Prove It: Fractions matter

For this drill you will need a piece of paper, a ruler, a pencil, and a penny. In one corner of the paper, make a tiny pencil point dot. That dot is your rear sight. About half an inch from the first dot, toward the center of the paper, make an identical dot. This second dot is your front sight. Now use the ruler and pencil to make a straight line through the center of both dots and continue the line across the entire paper. This straight line is the bullet path of your perfectly sighted shot.

Make another tiny dot immediately beside your front sight dot (you may let them touch). This dot represents an imperfectly aligned front sight. Use the ruler again to make a second line through the rear and new front sight dots, extending to the edge of the paper.

Now we will use the penny to pretend that you were aiming at a target nearly twice the size of your handgun. Center your penny (target) on the perfect bullet path. As you slide the penny away from the sights, you are changing target distance. Notice how little distance it takes to move the target completely off the imperfectly sighted bullet path. At the end of the paper, note how many target widths the improperly sighted round has moved away from the properly sighted bullet path.

You have proven that every fraction of an inch matters.

FORECASTING BULLET PLACEMENT

To understand the principles of good sighting, it is helpful to consider military-style match shooting. In many of these events, a shooter will fire a rifle from 200 to 500 yards (or more) without telescopic sights. Each competitor keeps a small book that contains illustrations of each target at each stage of fire. These small, illustrated targets have a graph superimposed on them, with each square representing 1 inch on the actual target. After the shooter fires a shot, he records on the small target in his book where he believes the round has struck. This is a remarkable feat. Rifle shooters are recording hits on a target they cannot possibly see (about a quarter-inch hole at a few hundred yards). The actual target is pulled down behind a dirt berm to enable range personnel to find the bullet hole and mark it with a large colored disk. Then the target is raised and the shooter is able to see and record where the shot actually hit.

Match shooters are able to forecast where their shots have struck with better than 90 percent accuracy. A match shooter will know whether he missed a shot before seeing the repaired target. How is that humanly possible?

Wherever the front sight tip last appeared within the rear sight and on the target (with properly adjusted sights), at the instant the round was fired, is where the round has struck.

If match shooters can call their shots beyond 500 yards, handgun shooters can certainly call shots at 25 yards. This tells us that a handgun shooter firing in poor visibility can correct shooting errors even without being able to see where previous rounds have struck.

PERCEIVED TARGET SIZE

Sighting is a matter of exactness. Visual information must be accurate in order to command the body concerning the physical manipulation of the handgun during the shooting process. Without an exact aiming goal, no exact shooting expectations are realistic.

Let me explain in terms of driving. If you intend to drive from New York to California to visit your sister in San Diego, you will have to intentionally *aim* for San Diego. I mean, what good would it do for you to hit California, only to wind up in Sacramento? You need to figuratively aim for a precise spot—your sister's driveway—before you leave New York.

When shooting, select an exact aiming point that appears the size of the front sight or smaller. The handgun is specifically designed and manufactured to provide mechanical accuracy, but that accuracy can only be achieved *when a target is selected that appears no larger than the front sight.*

The popular man-size silhouettes are too large for close-range sighting, but the top half of the "x" in the center of those targets may appear to be the size of the front sight at about 10 yards. The entire silhouette will appear to be the size of the front sight at 100 yards. If a shooter aims for a 6-inch black bull's-eye at 15 yards and hits it, nothing is known of the shooter's competence and therefore the shooter can make no improvement. Hitting a 6-inch disk at 15 yards may mean you are a perfect shot. It may also mean that at 50 yards you will miss your mark by 15 feet. Aim for something that appears no larger than your front sight and you will have a useable measure of your shooting accuracy.

A cheap and excellent training tool can be had by using the blank side of a full-size target. Use a large black magic marker to draw a cross (the paper will comfortably hold six 6 x 6-inch crosses). The exact intersection of that cross will be easily recognizable out to about 20 yards; beyond that, simply draw the cross a little larger to increase visibility. You will discover almost immediately that your

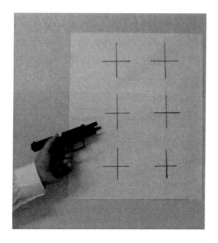

The world's best marksmanship target: blank paper and magic marker crosses. Saves money, too.

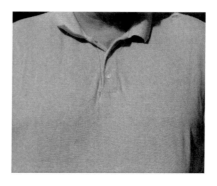

"Real life" aiming points. The front of this plain shirt has stains, seams, string, and buttons, which may all serve as aiming points no larger than the front sight tip. (Note: The best choices in this example would be the lower button or horizontal seam below it.)

group sizes shrink when you select a front sight-size aiming point.

This is where the "combat" shooting crowd may be tempted to claim that such techniques are unrealistic for defensive shooting. I disagree. Instead of letting your front sight drift inside of your attacker's blue shirt, select a button, coffee stain, or something else that appears no larger than your front sight. This technique is used by the best military and law enforcement snipers in the world. If you don't aim exactingly, you have no right to expect exact results. When no specific aiming point is possible (no button, no coffee stain, etc.), proper sighting will still enable you to better maintain a center mass aiming point by constant and exact measurement of the front sight tip against the rear sight and target.

Prove It: Front sight tip focus does not prevent "seeing" the target
You will need an ink pen and mirror (or other re-

flective surface) to complete this drill. Move back at least several feet (yards are better). Face the reflection and extend your shooting arm with the pen in your hand. Keeping the pen pointed up, use the end of it as your front sight tip. Focus intently on the front sight tip and superimpose it on your reflection. Do not focus on the reflection. Move your other arm and step side to side. Notice how clearly you can discern out-of-focus target identity, action, and movement.

You have proven that front sight focus does not "blind" the marksman.

SIGHTING FOR CONTROL AND CORRECTION

It has been stated a few times in this chapter that proper sighting allows the shooter to self-coach and control the entire shooting process. Here is how.

When proper sight alignment and proper sight picture are maintained with a fanatical discipline, every marksmanship error can be detected before the round is fired. An error is any action by the shooter that causes a bullet to strike other than the intended point of aim. Therefore, *all marksmanship errors are sighting errors* because the front sight (and muzzle) always points where the bullet will travel—a jerked trigger becomes a sighting error because it must move the front sight in order to cause the bullet to strike away from the point of aim. Otherwise, we have no error and hit our intended aiming point. Do you see? The front sight is the secret to controlling bullet placement, because no imperfection in the marksmanship process can escape detection if the shooter is focused on the front sight.

In the earlier example of a right-handed shooter who overgrips the handgun, as the muzzle turns down and left, the front sight tip will correspondingly turn down and left within the image of the out-of-focus rear sight. What does the shooter do with that information? Stop pressing the trigger, correct the overgrip, and regain perfect sighting. Error correction is that simple.

QUICK-FIRE METHODS

Unquestionably, proper sighting takes time. Perhaps less than a second, sometimes much more, but it always requires time. In cases where a shooter has no choice but to shoot quicker than he can fully acquire perfect sight alignment and perfect sight picture, he may use a faster sighting technique the United States Marine Corps calls "hasty sight picture." Quickly focus on the front sight, but require only that it stay within the vertical confines of the rear sight. This allows and increases the vertical spread of shots but will limit shots from wandering off the target when properly executed.

Hasty sight picture is useable as a *quick-fire* and *close-range technique* for handgun shooting. Col. Jeff Cooper advocated a similar technique, "flash sight picture." These techniques are valuable but are not alternatives for proper sighting when used beyond their intended purpose. Even these excellent quick-fire methods, when properly executed, require a determined focus on the front sight tip; otherwise, the shooter is just hoping to hit his mark and not strike unintended targets.

LIGHT AND COLOR

Sighting can be influenced, particularly as distances increase beyond 50 yards, by light and color. For instance, on a very sunny day, light colors will appear to "bleed" onto darker colors. In dark weather the opposite may occur. This can present a sighting challenge if the shooter is using the dividing edge between two colors as a point of aim.

The answer is proper sight picture, which accepts the target as a blurred whole and minimizes the strain and mirage effect suffered when the focus drifts onto the target. During long-range shooting under bright light or failing light, when point-of-aim distortion has occurred, drop the sights from the target while keeping proper sight alignment. Raise the front sight back to the desired aiming point while maintaining tip focus. This will alleviate most long-range light and color distortion.

MOVING TARGETS

The scope of this book is the Fundamentals of Marksmanship, but a brief word about moving targets is worthwhile. Shooting at a moving target can be frustrating because the shooter must fire at the location the target *will be* rather than where the target *is* at the time the trigger is pulled. "Tracking" is following the target with perfect sight alignment. There is a strong temptation for the shooter to stop tracking at the point the trigger pull is completed. The tracking swing must be smooth and continual throughout the shooting process, similar to shooting clay pigeons with a shotgun. The point of aim or "hold" depends on distance, target speed, and ballistics, which, unfortunately, is more than we are able to discuss here. A *very general rule* for handgun shooting at a moving target at less than 40 yards is "one second ahead," which in some cases will be the leading edge and, on very slow targets, the leading half of the object at which you are aiming.

QUESTIONS AND ANSWERS ABOUT SIGHTING

Q1: How can a person with less than perfect vision acquire perfect sighting?

A1: You only need clear vision to the front sight tip. The target, regardless of distance, must appear out of focus. Most vision problems do not prevent good marksmanship. If your target is a garbage can lid and you have proper sighting, it will appear blurred. The garbage can lid will not look like a horse, a refrigerator, or a station wagon; it will simply be a gray, round object for which you are able to determine the edges and the center. Don't forget to wear your glasses.

Q2: Why not change my focus back and forth between the target and the front sight for better control?

A2: There is no benefit to focusing on the target while shooting. The target is completely visible to the shooter when out of focus. When the target is in focus, the front sight is out of focus and, of course, the front sight is always moving. When focus leaves the front sight tip, the sights will move from the aiming point. There is nothing to be gained by leaving the front sight tip and everything to lose.

Q3: What if the target is moving? Shouldn't I focus on it then?

A3: Absolutely not. Even if your target moves at several miles an hour, you can track it perfectly while it is blurred. A running deer seen in focus or out of focus maintains shape and center of mass. More importantly, the exactness required to align sights and targets creates a constant high-speed problem for the shooter. In addition to the body's constant movement, sighting on a moving target requires the shooter to exceed the speed of the target in order to track and lead it. In other words, your sights are going to move about at a speed greater than your target. Stay on the tip.

Q4: Isn't this all pointless once I install a laser sight or electronic sight?

A4: Sighting with a laser is extremely difficult if the shooter is chasing the dot. As the body moves the laser moves. Because the red dot is easy to acquire at very close range, there is a temptation for the shooter to forgo proper sighting. That mistake will become apparent at longer distances, where the laser dot tends to bounce around the countryside. However, if you use your mechanical sights to acquire sight alignment and sight picture, you can find your laser dot instantly and every time. A laser is simply another front sight tip (a wonderful front sight tip that can be seen in the dark). The same exactness used with mechanical sights must be applied to the electronic sight. Lasers and electronic sights are wonderful additions, but they will not improve your shooting any more than would a new set of grips unless the fundamentals are applied. There is no "fix" for poor marksmanship other than good marksmanship.

Q5: My sights don't adjust. How do I figure out how to adjust my aiming point for wind and elevation?

A5: In the training section of this book, you will find drills to develop your long-range shooting skills. In general, you train for it by using a precise target that allows you to check your drop (vertical) and drift (horizontal). You need to deliberately educate yourself on the range. There is no single formula (that I am aware) to cover all distances, all handguns, and all ammunition.

Q6: What difference does it make whether I think trigger control is more important than sighting, as long as I do both correctly?

A6: If your house was burning, would you rush inside to save both your newborn child and goldfish with equal enthusiasm? Both goals may be "correct," but priorities matter.

Q7: Why do my shots land all around my aiming point when I'm sure I have good sighting?

A7: At the last instant, your eye is leaving the tip and moving to the target. There are some techniques in the training portion of this book that will help you. Keep your eye on the front sight tip for one second after the round has been fired. This "follow-through" will help you control your wandering eye. Remember, if you did not see the sight move, it is because you were not watching.

Q8: What do you mean when you say the body is in constant movement?

A8: Circulation, respiration, and muscular tension move the body even when "still." If you watch someone sleeping, you will notice that person still moves—the torso expands and retracts with breathing. Once you pick up a firearm, it is in constant movement. And remember: fractions of an inch matter.

Q9: I watch my front sight and have good sight alignment and sight picture, so why do my shots go all over the target?

A9: You are *not* focusing on your front sight tip. If you were, you would see the front sight move out of alignment and off the target. It could be that you are jerking your trigger faster than you can monitor through the sights. The next chapter addresses that problem.

Q10: My front sight tip keeps moving. What can I do about it?

A10: You can read the next chapter, which discusses managing natural movement. The movement is always with the shooter, but it can be minimized and controlled. Your focus is correct—keep watching the front sight tip.

Q11: I can't tell where my front sight tip ends and the target begins in bright sunlight. How do I minimize reflection off the tip?

A11: Use a felt-tip black magic marker to darken and dull your front sight tip, or try some commercial sight blackening. The old range smudge pots work great, too.

Q12: How much eye relief should I have?

A12: That depends on your arm length and stance. In general, more eye relief provides a more exacting perspective with which to align the sights. Many match shooters prefer to shoot one-handed just to gain another inch or so of eye relief, and likewise, two-handed defensive shooters benefit from a naturally straight shooting arm.

SUMMARY

If marksmanship is an airliner, proper sighting is the flight deck. The entire shooting process can be controlled by the shooter fanatically watching a crystal-clear front sight tip and making adjustments based on information received from the sights. Sighting is a discipline in which there can be no compromise. Your reward for intensity will be conversion from just another hapless shooter into an independent marksman. If you want to shoot well, master the principles of proper sighting.

CHAPTER THREE

☆☆☆☆☆

TRIGGER CONTROL AND GRIP (HANDS)

Think of the four fundamentals in terms of military life. Sight alignment is leadership principles, code of conduct, and knowledge of general orders. Body alignment and natural point of aim is military deportment. Breathing is military courtesy. But trigger control and grip is a lot of painting rocks, running in place with a rifle over your head, and getting your rear-end kicked up around your ears . . . you really need to participate to enjoy the benefits.

Trigger control and grip, like the other fundamentals, requires intellectualizing marksmanship; uniquely, it also requires the education of "feel." A shooter desiring to master the second fundamental of marksmanship will have to add experience to knowledge, physical skill to understanding. The discipline of the hands is the most difficult of the Fundamentals of Marksmanship because it requires more dedication than the average shooter is usually willing to provide.

PRESSURE AND MOVEMENT

Grip is the shooter's first intrusion into the perfection of the inanimate handgun. Left to itself, the handgun will fire to exactly the point at which it is aimed (omitting mechanical, ballistic, and environmental limitations and influences). The handgun *needs* a shooter to acquire a target. It does not need a shooter to make it motionless. Of course, the human element is the only reason we have extraneous physical movement during the firing sequence.

As discussed in the previous chapter, the eye is making decisions within hundredths of an inch, but it is the hand that has to execute the adjustments. Most of what the hand must do during shooting concerns aligning the sights because of extraneous movement; otherwise, the shooter would align the sights once before firing and no further alignment would be necessary. *Constant body movement requires constant sight alignment.* Unnecessary movement is the enemy of marksmanship. While the hand is not the sole cause of disruptive motion, it is nearly always complicit. The hand is both cause and cure.

We know physical pressure influences the handgun; if the shooter pushes from the right side, the handgun will point left. Nearly every shooter improperly uses his hands by overpressuring the trigger and the handgun. Consider the handgun as an object. It sits perfectly still on the range table. When the hand picks it up, the handgun becomes an object in constant motion. The motion is not severe by normal standards, but by marksmanship standards the sights are in constant and chaotic flux.

The human being holding a handgun has learned over a lifetime that objects that move can be stopped by physical pressure. When a book falls off a shelf, he grabs it. When a coin rolls near the edge of a table, he slaps it still. Because of these experiences, and from popular culture myths about recoil, our shooter will overgrip his weapon. If you have a cell phone that weighs 6 ounces, will you hold it with 10 pounds of pressure? If you do, you will find it rather difficult to punch in a telephone number because your phone will be shaking. Pressure is energy. *Energy delivered to your handgun beyond what is required to prevent it from moving between shots will become handgun movement.* If you squeeze your handgun beyond what is necessary, that additional energy must be dispersed. Since the shooter outweighs the handgun, the handgun will receive the energy and disperse it through movement.

Prove It: Less pressure equals less movement

This exercise will spill water on the ground, so it is advisable to conduct this drill outdoors. You will need an empty soup can with no lid attached and no jagged edges. Fill the can to the brim with water. In this exercise, the can represents the handgun and the water serves as sight alignment. The goal will be to get the can/handgun as still as possible for perfect sight alignment.

Gripping the can with your shooting hand, extend your arm away from your body. Do not lock your elbow. You will see the can moving. Gradually *increase* your grip (do not crush the can), using more and more strength to squeeze the can. Try to use your strength to keep the can from moving. Stop when water is spilled.

Since your sight alignment has hit the ground, refill the can with water. Again, grip the can with your shooting hand and extend your arm as before. Watch the can. Now *lighten* your grip until movement is reduced.

You have just proven that most movement can be eliminated by *reducing* grip, and additional pressure does not "steady" the handgun but further destabilizes it.

SHOOTING HAND GRIP

To shoot most handguns, including most magnums and large-bore service pistols, the only physical contact points required to prevent dropping the weapon are the pad of the trigger finger and the web of the shooting hand (between thumb and trigger finger). That is all that is necessary to fire a handgun accurately—once. The other fingers of the shooting hand are not needed to prevent dropping the handgun; the trigger finger and web of the hand will hold on to the weapon through recoil. The additional fingers merely keep the weapon from shifting between shots. Recoil can slide the handgun; the other three fingers of the shooting hand maintain proper control during a string of fire (we will cover recoil in the chapter on body alignment and natural point of aim). *If your fingertips turn red and white when gripping your handgun, you are overgripping.* There should be virtually no discoloration of the fingertips during firing.

You would not hold an office stapler with enough pressure to drain the blood from your fingertips. Why do it with a handgun? A centerfire rifle does not have sufficient power to knock a man down. If a man wore sufficient body armor to resist penetration by a rifle round, he would not be moved by the impact. Further, we can concede to Mr. Newton that an explosion, as occurs when a firearm is discharged, expels energy in opposite directions. Energy pushes out of the muzzle and back against the shooter. If a round could knock down a man by force of impact, the recoil from that round would also knock down the shooter.

Why does any of this matter to marksmen? It matters because if the energy from a rifle cannot move a person, a handgun, with a fraction of that same force, certainly is not able to overpower a shooter. So, the handgun and the office stapler should be held in similar fashion, with no more pressure than necessary to retain them while shooting—or stapling.

The alignment of the hand and firearm is based on the barrel. The grip should seat the handgun straight into the web of the shooting hand, putting the bones of the forearm in line with the barrel. In this way, we imitate the stability of the rifle by providing a straight line of support to the shoulder. The position of the shooting hand is as high on the backstrap as possible without going above the trigger.

In almost all cases, particularly with pistols, the shooter will not be able to go above the trigger, though I mention it because it may be possible on some small revolvers. The trigger finger, when extended to the trigger, must be level. This high position on the grips of the handgun is done to minimize recoil, and therefore the time needed to recover sighting between shots, and to provide general stability throughout the shooting sequence. Additionally, a high grip shortens the distance between the hand and the trigger, requiring less reach with the trigger finger.

Consider a man lying on a weight bench performing dumbbell flies with his arms fully extended. He will perceive the dumbbells to be heavier than if he bends his arms and brings the weights closer to his body. Likewise, the trigger finger will be "stronger" and have greater control when the distance to the trigger is shortened. The reason this phenomenon occurs in shooting is because the grip portion of the handgun frame slants or bends toward the trigger. In the case of revolvers, the grips are usually narrower at the top. A high, straight hold on the handgun is the basis for successful trigger control and grip.

Prove It: High grip equals control

For this exercise you will need a broom or mop handle. The broom handle will be the handgun. Your support hand will simulate recoil. Grip the broom about 2 feet below the end of the handle with your shooting hand. Hold it as tightly as you can. Use your support hand to lightly pull the tip of the broom handle toward you. You will notice that despite how hard you grip with your shooting hand, your support hand can easily move the broom handle.

Try the exercise again, but this time, grip the broom handle 4 inches from the top. Now use your support hand to lightly pull on the 4 inches of broom handle exposed above the shooting hand. Notice the shooting hand now controls the broom handle.

You have proven that high hand placement minimizes the effects of recoil.

OVERGRIP TORQUE

The muscular pressure generated by overgripping the weapon brings an additional problem beyond extraneous movement—torque. When the shooting hand overgrips, it does so with a twisting force, downward and inward. When pressure is applied to the clenched fist, the hand naturally rotates in and down. The movement can be resisted, of course, but the natural movement is not a bend at the wrist; it is a twist that turns the right hand to about eight o'clock and the left hand to about four o'clock (this applies to both single- and two-handed shooting). This error is so widespread that if you meet a fellow shooter for the first time and can determine whether he is right- or left-handed, you can predict his major marksmanship error with startling accuracy. If he is a right-hander, say, "I bet you have a problem with your shots going low left, at about seven or eight o'clock—even when you hit inside the bull's-eye." You will be right nine times out of ten.

Many years ago, the FBI came up with a flashlight shooting technique that required the agent to hold his flashlight in the left hand while extending the left arm away from the body. Then the agent would lunge to his right into a combat crouch for single-handed firing. The intent was to trick bad guys into shooting at the flashlight instead of the agent. That technique lost support when it was discovered that bad guys, the majority of whom are also right-handed, tend to overgrip their handguns. So naturally, when they aimed at the flashlights, their shots went low and left, striking the agents.

Prove It: Overgrip is torque

For this exercise you will need a few sheets of paper, some transparent tape, a writing pen, and a smooth horizontal surface (e.g., wall or door). Tape the paper to the wall a few sheets thick to make a better writing surface and to protect the wall. Make a fist with your shooting hand and wedge the un-capped pen between the shooting and middle fingers. The writing point must be facing outward with the majority of the pen visible. Make certain that the butt of the pen is seated securely inside the fist, against the palm of your hand. The result should be that the pen points similar to the way a handgun barrel would point when held by your shooting hand.

Without locking your elbow, fully extend your shooting arm and allow the point of the pen to press against the paper. Instantly tighten your hand as if snatching an object with your fist. In other words, squeeze as hard as you can, as fast as you can.

Examine the mark made by the pen. If you did this exercise right-handed, you made a mark heading low left. If you did it with your left hand, your mark went low right.

You have proven that the shooting hand, when overgripping, torques down to the inside. Don't over-grip. It is unnecessary for retaining the weapon, and it destroys accuracy.

We have talked about the disease, now we will discuss the cure.

THUMBS

The thumbs are the marksmanship version of tonsils—nice to have, but you'll probably need to remove them. The shooting-hand thumb can work great mischief on accuracy. The thumb does not press directly back against the opposing fingers and therefore provide countermovement, as some believe. Rather, the thumb creates a downward and inward pressure, resulting in a spiraling barrel movement to the non-shooting side. In other words, the thumb plays a predominant role in the problem of shooting-hand torque.

Daily experience has taught you that when you wish to grip something for maximum hold, you wrap four fingers around one side and your thumb around the other, like gripping a hammer. The thumb provides leverage for overgrip. But do we need the thumb(s) to grip the handgun during firing? No. Remember, we only use the non-shooting fingers to prevent displacement in between shots. We do not need to use the thumbs. *By simply lifting your thumbs off the weapon, you will dramatically reduce your tendencies toward strong-hand torque.*

Top view of two-hand grip with thumbs off frame.

Single-hand grip properly indexing with thumb off the frame. (Note: Thumb is lifted but not hyperextended.)

Two-hand grip with thumbs off and away from revolver cylinder.

Two-hand grip with thumbs off while firing revolver.

Firing a pistol with two hands allows both thumbs to be lifted off the weapon at about a 45-degree angle, lightly touching, side by side. Likewise, single-handed shooting allows for the shooting thumb to be lifted off the weapon. Thumbs off the handgun must be relaxed; straining can cause a degree of torque. An added benefit to firing without thumbs is an instant correction for a shooter who tends to put shots exactly centerline of the aiming point but an inch or two toward the non-shooting side. This occurs because in addition to causing torque, the shooting thumb can provide leverage for the trigger finger to push the handgun to the non-shooting side. Thumbs cause mischief; lift them up!

TWO-HAND GRIP

Handguns were brought forward for the convenience of one-handed firing. It likely would have been amusing to our predecessors to know that we use two hands for controlling a handgun. It was logical to think of the pistol as a single-handed tool, because one-handed firing capability was the technical breakthrough that the pistol offered. Drawings from the 1700s through photographs of mid-19th century America show a form of handgun shooting that allowed for great movement of the wrist to disperse recoil and an upright stance freed from the constriction of stocked weapons.

At the beginning of this book, I stated that very little had changed over the years concerning human knowledge of marksmanship. That is true, but a major change in shooting technique did occur in the mid-20th century when handguns became two-handed weapons. In the old days, policing was far less intrusive in public life. Officers of the law were more reactive and in less need of portable and concealable weapons. Swords and other bladed instruments were much more practical for close range than a longarm and much more reliable than early pistols. Also, bladed weapons and even blunt objects could be used "rapid fire"; not so with a muzzle-loading, single-shot pistol.

In the Old West, no man would choose to travel across the open range with a "sidearm" if a rifle was available. Today, we would agree with the old cowboys as far as selecting the best tool for the job. Where we likely would differ is in how we view the handgun. In the modern, more urbanized age, wherein hunting is less and less a birthright and the physical limits of personal property are much smaller, the handgun has replaced the rifle as the primary weapon in many homes. The first choice for many defensive shooters is the handgun, and the safest, most practical way to shoot a handgun is with two hands.

SUPPORT HAND

Every defensive shooter must train to safely manipulate and accurately fire the handgun with the support hand. Use this book to train yourself to fire with both hands.

But what is the support hand's role in two-handed shooting? The proper use of the shooting hand has already been discussed. *The support hand is the single element that provides the benefit of two-handed shooting.* Unfortunately, the majority of shooters get very little benefit from the support hand, and in some cases, the support hand negatively impacts their shooting.

There is a common misunderstanding about what the support hand is intended to provide. Most shooters assume the primary function is to "steady" the firearm. That is incorrect. *The primary function of the support hand is to provide a load-bearing platform that enables the shooting hand to shift from weightlifting to sight alignment adjustments and trigger press.* When you master the support hand, you will, in effect, be shooting single-handed from inside a supportive rest.

The shooting hand has only two goals: to continually maneuver the handgun into perfect sight alignment and sight picture, and to execute an efficient and nondisruptive trigger press. That is the physical "meat" of marksmanship. To additionally task the shooting hand with weight bearing is foolish and counterproductive.

The loaded handgun weighs about 3 to 6 pounds, which is a lot of weight to support at arm's length. Bull's-eye shooters firing single-handed do it remarkably well with a natural and relaxed posture. Unfortunately, most two-handed shooters make the task difficult by using the shooting arm to also support the non-shooting hand. Most shooters will latch onto the shooting hand with the non-shooting hand. This error transfers a portion of the support-arm weight with all the weight of the supporting hand onto the shooting hand. Consequently, the shooting arm is literally weightlifting during the shooting sequence. The fix is simple enough. *The supporting hand lifts the handgun and shooting hand.*

Regardless of stance, the supporting hand should bear the majority of the weight. Here is how you can free your shooting hand for sight alignment and perfect trigger control:

---

1. Place the butt of your handgun in your supporting palm. The goal here is not a "cup and saucer" grip but simply to have a portion of the supporting palm providing vertical (weight bearing) support. The exact location of where the butt of the handgun will be placed depends upon the size ratio of hand versus handgun. Smaller hands will need to place the butt near the edge of the supporting hand. Personal preference and comfort matter here, too. Remember, the goal is weight support; gathering up the shooting hand with a bit of the handgun butt will accomplish your purpose. Avoid using side compression because that will bring you into overgrip.

Two-hand grip, #1. First, set the pistol into the edge of the supporting palm. (Note: Exact placement of the handgun butt into the palm is determined by the relative size of hand versus handgun.)

2. Wrap the remainder of the supporting hand around the shooting hand, keeping the thumbs together. The supporting hand becomes a reverse of the shooting hand, with the fingers following the same line but from an opposite direction.

Do not run your supporting fingers vertically against the horizontal grip of your shooting hand. They won't align perfectly, but they ought not to be perpendicular. Such a platform is less stable and awkward under speed.

Thumbs go together, even with revolvers. If you haven't yet learned, crossing your thumbs will get you a nasty scrape from a rearward traveling pistol slide. A revolver hammer can also get in a few digs. More importantly, "thumbs together" joins the heels of both hands, creating a more stable platform. Thumbs crossed kicks the heels outward, forming a triangular space between the hands.

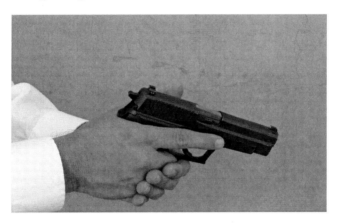

Two-hand grip, #2. Second, wrap the supporting "up and around" the shooting hand. (Note: The object is weight-bearing support, not crushing the shooting hand.)

3. Now lift with the supporting hand until the weight is removed from the shooting arm. Marksmanship serves the shooter and not the other way around. Some marksmen will not be able to use the support arm to relieve the shooting arm of all weight-bearing responsibilities. Follow the intent of the principle as far as possible; observance to any degree will benefit the shooter. Now, friend, you are ready for some good trigger control and the management of natural motion . . .

Two-hand grip, #3. Third, lift the supporting arm and transfer the weight of the shooting hand and firearm to the supporting hand/arm.

Firing with the two-hand grip.

MANAGING NATURAL SIGHT MOVEMENT

We know that holding a handgun causes that handgun to be in motion. Further, we have proven that extraneous pressure causes additional unwanted movement. The reader has discovered how to eliminate surplus pressure on the handgun. But what about the natural movement that occurs even when a marksman properly grips a handgun? Heartbeat, respiration, and muscular tension are always present in marksmanship. In later chapters, we will look at sources of motion beyond the hand, but there is an easy method to control natural and unavoidable front sight movement.

The "figure 8" is an old marksmanship technique long used to manage "sight wobble." Instead of allowing the front sight to wander all over the great outdoors, the shooter guides the front sight into a figure 8, with the center of the 8 superimposed on the point of aim. Try this with a horizontal 8 first. A vertical 8 will work well, too, but I think the vertical is better for rifle or long-range shooting and the horizontal better for most handgun purposes. This is merely a personal preference. The object is to guide the disorganized movement into a predictable path that rhythmically intersects with the point of aim. Obviously, the point of aim pass-over point is the window for firing. The smaller the 8, the better the results; using too much space can create movement within your 8, and then you are back to where you started. Always remember that this technique should never rush your shot. If you aren't ready, wait for the next pass over.

TRIGGER FINGER PLACEMENT

There is a rule in shooting that advises shooters to use the pad of the trigger finger for pistols and the first joint of the trigger finger for revolvers. That isn't a bad rule, but here is a much better one: *Understand what the trigger finger needs to accomplish and then position it to accomplish that task.*

Hold your hand out in front of you and move your index/trigger finger. Notice the trigger finger naturally closes like a swinging gate. It moves in a downward arc. Think for a moment; is that movement compatible with maintaining sight alignment? Do you want an angled pressure applied to your handgun during shooting? (If you do, then you've just been flipping through this book looking for pictures.) It may seem to the reader that direction of pressure does not matter, because the trigger is a mechanical switch that will move rearward regardless of the angle at which it is engaged. Regrettably, *the trigger does not automatically travel straight to the rear.* A perfect, neutral-influence trigger path requires deliberate action.

If you examine a completely safe handgun, taking the trigger between your thumb and forefinger, you will discover the trigger allows lateral movement—it can be moved from side to side. Therefore, the shooter must act deliberately to bring the trigger straight back without lateral deviation. So, when placing the trigger finger on the trigger, position your finger to bring the trigger straight to the rear without pressing or pulling to either side. A trigger can push to the

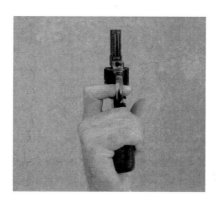

Proper trigger press at the start. (Note: Finger is moved out of the trigger guard to fit this shooter's hand.)

Proper trigger press at the firing. (Note: The goal is a straight back movement. Hand-to-firearm fit may not allow perfect rearward movement—experiment to find your best fit.)

support side and, by curling around the trigger face, pull to the shooting side.

The preferred seating of the trigger finger tip, pad, or joint is one that allows the trigger finger to bend above the middle knuckle to allow the entire finger to produce a virtually straight rearward press. Fit of the hand to the firearm will determine how much finger goes into the trigger guard. Understand that your goal is a straight-to-the-rear, neutral-influence trigger press. Think of what you are trying to accomplish when you position the weapon in your hand. And now for the hard part . . .

TRIGGER PRESS

Imagine a child's wagon filled to the brim with water. Now, without spilling a drop, gently *push* the little wagon over a very narrow and bumpy cobblestone bridge. That, I regret to inform you, is the image of a good trigger press with a service-grade pistol. Proper trigger control requires knowledge, experience (proper practice as described in detail in the training chapter of this book), sensitivity, and a surprising amount of patience—all of which are well within the grasp of the average shooter.

It is essential for the aspiring marksman to understand "trigger pull." The term suggests the trigger finger and adjoining muscles of the hand pulling the trigger rearward. That is not what is needed for neutral influence and sensitive control during the rearward travel of the trigger. For the sake of clarity and because words have meaning, I hope the reader will indulge me in referring to "trigger pull" as "trigger press." The physical motivation for the rearward motion of the trigger must come from the trigger finger and not the hand. It is a push—not a pull. You may be tempted to accuse me of playing non-sensical word games, but indulge me for a bit.

When the trigger is properly used, it will be isolated from the rest of the hand. The finger will have to press, having minimized leverage with the hand. Your trigger finger has more than enough muscle to bring the trigger home. The problem that most often occurs is the muscles of the forearm, hand, and fingers overpower the trigger. Everything you have read in this chapter has brought you to an isolated trigger finger free to do one thing—a perfect trigger press.

TAKE-UP

There is some mechanical slack at the beginning of the trigger travel in almost every handgun. This poses no real difficulty for the shooter who knows what to expect. The trigger finger will simply gather the slack before beginning the actual press against trigger tension. Keep your trigger press fast and tidy by automatically gathering the slack and holding on to it after the shot has been fired (which we will discuss further below).

STAGING, CONTINUITY, AND CONTROL

The distance the trigger travels after take-up is, depending on your handgun, often full of bumps, snags, and uneven resistance. Obviously, target-grade pistols are much smoother than service-grade pistols, but trigger press is rarely buttery smooth. The key to success is a continual and evenly applied pressure that increases to match trigger resistance. Naturally, the marksman subordinates the trigger press to sighting. If sight alignment is compromised or if sight picture is corrupted, the shooting sequence must be stopped to prevent a missed shot. In all cases, the shooter is constantly adjusting the position of the weapon based on information from the sights. Most of these adjustments continue during trigger press. *In the case of an error that apparently cannot be corrected during trigger press, the solution is to release trigger pressure (not take-up) and begin afresh.* Unfortunately, what usually occurs is "staging."

Staging is pausing in the middle of a trigger press before continuing with the shot. In theory, this seems like a reasonable idea. In reality, it just does not work. During staging, the trigger finger loses sensitivity and strength, which tends to cause an excess in trigger pressure when the press resumes. There is an increased possibility for an unintentional discharge by loss of sensitivity through a sort of trigger finger "numbing." *Trigger press is a movement, not a position*. Avoid staging.

Proper trigger press never exceeds the shooter's ability to control the shooting process through sighting. *If the trigger is pressed faster than the shooter can monitor the sights, it becomes destructive to marksmanship*. This is not to say that trigger press must be slow. On the contrary, competition speed shooters have lightning-fast trigger press (matched by lightning-fast sighting).

Over many years I have watched countless shooters during the process of trigger press. Less than 5 percent of all shooters actually control the trigger to the point of mechanical release. Instead, most shooters pull the trigger just under three-quarters of the way toward release and then yank as quickly as they can. I think this is done because the shooter assumes he is near the end of the pull and wants a quick, clean release. However, no matter how fast one pulls the trigger, the length of the pull remains the same. To state it differently, you can hurry the shooting process, but you cannot shortcut the shooting process. If a shooter does not control the handgun throughout the entire range of trigger press, aiming is literally a matter of chance.

At the point when the trigger is yanked, sighting is abandoned and bullet placement is left to a thousand minute details that make up that brief uncontrolled instant. (In the training section of this book there are exercises to assist you in achieving a full, controlled trigger press and avoid flinching.) *The object is to have perfect sight alignment and perfect sight picture when the firing pin strikes the primer*. That is the reason we study marksmanship.

Emotion plagues us. There is a natural anticipation in waiting for the hammer to drop. That in itself is not a problem; the problem is the physical reaction that accompanies the anticipation. We do not want to tense ourselves or jerk muscles waiting for the "bang." Muscular tension is no friend to a sensitive trigger press. So let's deceive ourselves, trying to press the trigger as far as possible *without* firing the weapon. *Be surprised when the hammer finally breaks free.* The hammer drop should be a small surprise to the shooter who took no precaution to be protected from the discharge. By the time the shot is felt and heard, the bullet will already be at rest downrange and beyond the shooter's ability to move it off course.

We "protect" ourselves by tensing the body. *By recognizing that the round being fired will not hurt us by noise or recoil, and by letting ourselves be relaxed and open, we avoid disrupting perfect sighting.* You must get to know, by feel, how much trigger travel is necessary before the handgun will fire. The odds are you have never controlled the entire trigger travel. It is not a question of how far back *must* the trigger go; rather, it is a question of how far back *may* the trigger go before the shot is fired.

Control every hair's-breadth of trigger travel and your sighting can be beautiful. Dry fire techniques as explained in the training chapter will be invaluable to you in getting to your know your trigger. Relax through the shot. Let yourself go.

OVERTRAVEL AND TRIGGER RESET

When the trigger has traveled far enough to the rear, the hammer will fall and the round will be fired. That is not the end, however, of available trigger travel. Some "overtravel" is present on almost all handguns. Some weapons have a screw (trigger stop) behind the trigger that may be brought forward to prevent overtravel.

What is the harm of overtravel, you ask? For one thing, it does nothing constructive, because the shot has already been fired. The real evil of overtravel is what it does to speed. Overtravel is measured in fractions of an inch, but in terms of time it may add, depending on weapon, 10 percent because of the additional distance the trigger will travel. That is 10 percent slower for the next shot. Fortunately, we can train ourselves not to succumb to overtravel; unfortunately, overtravel is not the greatest enemy of trigger speed.

TRIGGER CONTROL AND GRIP (HANDS)

Trigger reset is simply the forward travel of the returning trigger necessary to begin a fresh trigger press. It is very easy to feel when trigger reset has been reached. It just takes training and practice. The difficulty arises because the trigger will go much farther forward than is actually necessary to reset the trigger. Unlike overtravel, this unnecessary forward travel may comprise more than 40 percent of the entire range of trigger movement. It gets worse. Many shooters will swing the trigger finger all the way forward, even removing it from the trigger face. It is not uncommon to see a shooter slap the inside of the trigger guard with his trigger finger. Not halting the trigger finger at the reset point could double your trigger time. *The good news: master trigger reset and fire up to twice as fast . . . twice as fast.*

QUESTIONS AND ANSWERS
ABOUT TRIGGER CONTROL AND GRIP

Q1: Will a light grip cause a failure to feed?

A1: No, but a limp wrist can cause failure to feed in some pistols, particularly those made expressly for target shooting. A light grip is not a limp wrist.

Q2: Why shouldn't I cross my thumbs to one side when revolver shooting?

A2: Because you're compressing your thumbs and may cause torque (depending on which side you place your thumbs), but you will certainly add pressure. If your shooting thumb crosses over your supporting thumb, you will likely break the weld between the heels of both hands. The thumbs aren't needed and neither is a death grip. A lighter grip and thumbs-free shooting is counterintuitive, so practice properly as outlined in the training chapter of this book.

Q3: Can't a light grip cause you to lose your handgun during a struggle?

A3: I fully endorse holding your handgun as hard as you can when someone is trying to steal it. That takes all of a split second and is no excuse not to properly handle your weapon. I understand that no one wants a bad guy to grab their gun, but you should realize that if anybody gets between your chest and your handgun, grip style will not be your greatest problem. This is a legitimate concern, but it is intellectually dishonest to suggest that proper grip and trigger control during shooting result in a handgun giveaway during a fight.

Q4: My instructor says a push/pull grip is necessary to "lock in" your weapon. Do you dispute that?

A4: You can't "lock in" a handgun because you can't prevent the body from moving as long as it is alive. "Lock in" is not a shooting technique—it's just a sales pitch. Challenge your instructor to a 50-yard bull's-eye contest. Watch to see what happens to the "push/pull," "combat thrust," "soda can crusher," "locked arm triangle," etc., etc. Likely, you'll discover your instructor doesn't mind practicing a little proper marksmanship when a steak dinner is on the line. The goal in all shooting is to hit your mark, and all I am advocating is accuracy. If real life is the concern (once again), how can we allow ourselves to only train at 15 yards or less? It isn't reasonable to assume that violent attackers will always enter our presence within spitting distance.

SUMMARY

The handgun does not twitch, shake, and wobble—you do. The less you interfere with the handgun, the better your ability to achieve perfect sighting. *Necessary* pressure that holds the handgun and presses the trigger must also be *neutral* pressure. The trigger is a bumpy, wobbling mechanical lever that requires a smooth, progressive press with no physical anticipation from the shooter. This Fundamental is the primary reason that perfect practice is a necessity. Remember, *the sights are master over the trigger—never apply pressure beyond what proper sighting can control,* or all of this is pointless.

CHAPTER FOUR

BODY ALIGNMENT AND
NATURAL POINT OF AIM (BODY)

Before the advent of the "science" of ergonomics, all we had was common sense. When they made the first automobiles, seats were installed facing forward so the driver would not have to turn his head. Saddles have been around for at least a thousand years and have always anticipated a forward-facing rider. Shirt buttons are on the front of the shirt, and shoes never lace at the heel. Mankind has always known that the human body functions best when it functions naturally. That is exactly the theme of this chapter.

BODY ALIGNMENT

The muscles of the body naturally function as a group of opposing springs. The torso can twist to one side by stretching muscles, but an opposite set of muscles are compressed by that same action. The only time this struggle of opposing tension does not occur is when the body is naturally positioned and therefore "loose." The living human body will attempt to right itself to a slack, neutral position. When you reach for a high shelf and feel the stretch up your legs, back, and arm, you are experiencing the body trying to return to a loose-muscle or neutral position. Think back to the last chapter— what type of physical presence is acceptable to the marksman? *Neu-*

67

tral influence enables the shooter to accomplish successful firing without driving the shooting process off course. Both the human body and the handgun want minimum interference. So, let's give them what they want.

Body alignment is the natural positioning of the body, avoiding directional muscular tension, to achieve a neutral position. Unless you are lying on your back, there will be some muscular tension. For instance, some muscular tension is required when standing to keep your knees from buckling and pitching you onto the floor. However, you will notice when standing, there is no counterpull within the body. The leg muscles may get tired of standing, but there is no muscular effort *against* standing. We can stand, then, and achieve a natural position. How does your body *prefer* to stand? I doubt you are comfortable waiting at a bus stop while standing on one foot or holding your arms over your head.

The body is designed to stand in this manner:

Feet apart and flat on the ground. The body-weight almost evenly dispersed between heels and balls of the feet (the heels, being directly under the body, get the lion's share of the weight, but the balls are under force to leverage body balance).

Legs straight without locking the knees. Locked knees are a hyperextension of the legs, which causes trembling. When legs are locked at the knees, they will seek to move at the next lowest joint, the ankles, which will cause the entire body to pitch like a ship's mast in a storm. This simple error can actually subject a handgun shooter to the effects of wind during a breeze that the shooter might not otherwise notice.

Hips even and canted naturally forward.
Tucking the pelvis may be good posture, but it is not
how the body naturally rests.

Back naturally straight. Do not stretch the
spine; it is naturally S shaped.

Arms hanging loosely to the sides. Hands rest
slightly forward, with the palms canted inward.

Neck almost straight. The head squared forward and almost imperceptibly pointing downward.

The above is the body's wish list for a natural standing position.
We will modify it slightly to accomplish marksmanship, and you will
have the perfect shooting stance.

NATURAL SHOOTING STANCE

There are a few popular two-handed shooting stances with several variations. I find two to be worthwhile. The first is the one we
have been working toward; let's call it the "natural stance." Here the
shooter simply faces the target head-on and stands naturally (with a
few gentle modifications).

Begin this stance from the natural standing position as previously
described. Add the following:

**1. Shoulder carriage is rolled *slightly* forward,
causing the arms to drop the hands just in front of
the thighs.** When executed correctly, this modifica-
tion will feel natural to the shooter and involves no
destructive muscular tension. Actually, this is simply a
posture of fatigue. The value of this position is that it
brings the shoulder carriage just slightly forward of

the waist. During firing, recoil will not get beyond the elbows and, in most cases, the hands. You may experience muzzle flip, but the recoil will not lift the shoulders if they are positioned properly. The arms are also brought closer together, giving the supporting arm needed length for a semivertical support (which you no doubt remember from the last chapter).

Typical standing posture with shoulders positioned in-line with the hips.

Converting to a good shooting posture. Shoulders are rolled forward of the hips, greatly reducing the effects of recoil and increasing the speed of follow-up shots.

Shoulders forward. (Note: The joints are relaxed, not locked.)

2. Arms are lifted in front of the body to eye height. The shooting arm is naturally straight (never locked, which restricts blood flow and causes trembling), and the support arm has a slight bend at the elbow, enabling the supporting hand to come up from underneath but still to the side of the shooting hand. Eye height is important, because if the eye is brought down to the weapon, eye relief is often lessened and perspective changed as the eye is rolled upward to see forward. In the sighting chapter (brilliantly written), we discussed using the dominant eye for sighting. A small percentage of shooters have a dominant eye and dominant hand that do not match. A crisscrossing of right eye and left hand, for instance, is easily compensated for using the natural stance. The shooter must never move the head but rather bring the hand across to the dominant eye. It is a natural adjustment, easily done with this stance. *The natural stance is suited to all body types.*

BLADED SHOOTING STANCE

The "bladed stance" is of particular value to law enforcement and others who carry holstered weapons. This stance keeps the holstered handgun away from the target and allows the shooter to assume foot placement similar to that of a boxer. The bladed stance lends itself to fending off blows and gun grabs.

Unlike the natural stance, the bladed stance does not work for all body types. Shooters with short arms and large chests will not be able to properly assume the bladed stance. One remedy is to lessen the angle of the shooter to the target. The cardinal sin against the bladed stance is twisting of the body. Proportionately shorter-limbed shooters will find it difficult to bring the shooting arm across the body without twisting the legs or torso. The answer is not to do an improper bladed stance but to execute a perfect natural stance. The bladed has no advantage over the natural beyond the defensive qualities already mentioned. Those advantages can be achieved with the natural stance through the incorporation of a little extra distance between defender and suspect.

Starting from the natural shooting stance, here is the best method to finding your bladed stance:

1. Move your shooting-side foot rearward to no more than 45 degrees from the target. Align the support-side foot with the shooting-side foot. The angle you choose is determined by your physique and comfort.

2. Keep the knees, hips, shoulders, and head in line with the feet and face downrange at exactly the same angle. It is essential that there be no twisting of the body. The result (so far) should be the shooter standing naturally in front of the target and angled toward the shooting side. This is the natural stance at this stage, with the difference being the shooter is not looking directly onto the target.

3. Keep the head upright and turn it toward the target. Now you have your body in the natural stance, angled in relation to the target, and your head directly facing the target.

Bladed stance. Feet, knees, hips, chest, and shoulders are angled away from the target. Head and arms alone shift to the target.

4. Raise the shooting arm out to shoulder height and swing it across the body until it is in line with the dominant eye. Only your shooting arm and head should be directly facing the target.

5. Raise the supporting arm and assume a proper supporting grip. The only muscular tension allowed in the bladed stance is that required to turn the head (neck) and the tensing of the shoulder muscle necessary to bring the shooting arm across the body. *There must be no tension in the legs or back.*

PRONE POSITION

Lying in the prone position will change your eye relief and perspective. That means you will shoot to a different point on your target. You must train in order to master each position. If you use the bladed stance, then use a bladed prone. If you use the natural stance, then use a straight, natural prone.

KNEELING POSITION

Like the prone, the kneeling must be mastered through training. I always found kneeling unstable, but not every shooter does. An alternative is to kneel with both knees, natural or bladed, which is simply standing at the knees.

Prove It: Proper distribution
of weight flattens recoil

I regret the only way this exercise can be done effectively is with the help of a second person. But one assistant is all that is needed. Assume a shooting stance with your hands gripped together (no handgun). Lean backward slightly. Have the assistant stand in front of you and place his overlapped and open hands about 4 inches in front of your grip. The assistant will give your double-fisted grip a short, light shove.

Now, do the same thing, but this time stand bolt upright—perfectly straight.

One more time, but in this case bring the shoulder carriage just slightly forward of the hips.

In the first case, you likely took a step backward to maintain your balance. This often occurs with shooters who lean back during firing. In the second example, you probably felt your weight rock back on your heels. Imagine what that would do to a follow-up shot.

In the last attempt, with a forward shoulder carriage, nothing happened. The same recoil that "knocked you back" in the first case and slowed you down in the second had no effect on you when your weight was properly distributed.

You have proven that the shooter determines the extent of recoil, not the handgun.

ARMS

In understanding arm placement, you need to know two things: hand placement and function (the last chapter) and how to avoid muscular tension (this chapter). From that you should understand how to position your arms. If the primary purpose of the supporting hand is weight bearing, then logically your supporting elbow would tend to point downward. I will give you a guideline for arm placement, but hopefully, you are beginning to see that *marksmanship is reasonable, logical, and therefore predictable*.

Imagine you are holding your pistol in a proper two-handed grip. Your target is a giant clock face. You are aiming dead center at the base of the clock arms. If you are a right-hander, your shooting elbow is pointed to about four o'clock and your supporting elbow is pointed to about seven o'clock. A left-hander has a shooting elbow to about eight o'clock and the supporting elbow is pointed to about five o'clock (never straight down). Notice the use of the word "about"; arm placement depends on physiognomy. Please remember: technique serves the shooter, not the other way around. You cannot have mastery of the Fundamentals of Marksmanship without understanding the "why" and then managing the "how."

NATURAL POINT OF AIM

We have learned that proper body alignment is the natural positioning of the body. "Natural point of aim" is using that good, "loose" body alignment and aiming the entire body at the target. We will aim the human as we aim the gun, relaxed and natural.

To learn natural point of aim, a shooter must start from the end and work backward. You have chosen your stance and you have acquired your grip. Now aim at your target by adjusting your body so that you have perfect sight alignment and sight picture, natural body position (natural stance or bladed stance), and, of course, no additional muscular tension. Here's how you test your natural point of aim.

Close your eyes after achieving perfect sighting. Keep your eyes closed for 5 or 10 seconds. Reopen your eyes and see whether your front sight drifted left or right. If your front sight moved to either side, you did not have good natural point of aim. *Muscles in the body will try to "correct" the body to the neutral or at-rest position. The marksman makes this natural centering of the body work to his advantage.* To correct natural point of aim errors, do not contort your body; simply shuffle your feet until you have repositioned the body in order to achieve natural point of aim on your target. Memorize this position in relation to your target. *Incorporate good natural point of aim into your shooting stance.* Without true natural point of aim, shots, particularly rapid fire, will be pulled in the direction of involuntary muscular correction. Good natural point of aim is not optional in marksmanship.

Prove It: Body alignment effects accuracy
Assume your preferred shooting stance and grip (no handgun needed). Lift up the shooting-hand thumb to serve as a front sight blade. Twist your torso to

your non-shooting side until you are aiming to the rear. Pick an aiming point the size of your thumb and acquire sight picture. Now shut your eyes and slowly count to 10. Open your eyes and regain sight picture.

You will notice that your body has involuntarily moved off target toward the shooting side. While the stance used was an exaggeration, there was no recoil to contend with during this exercise. Simply standing with stretched muscles puts the shooter at odds with his body. During this exercise, you felt the pull of calf, thigh, back, shoulder, neck, and arm muscles. In the future, let that feeling of muscular tension be a warning that natural body alignment has not been acquired.

You have proven that body position is an integral part of the sighting process.

MUSCLES

Muscles are movement. Blood races through them and nerves make them twitch. Everything you have learned about gripping the handgun applies to a much greater degree when considering the influence of the human body on marksmanship. Never lock joints; this is unnatural, causes trembling, and restricts blood flow. Likewise, never flex muscles while shooting, again, causing movement.

CROUCHING TIGERS

There are many instructors who teach students to assume a deliberate crouching position when firing. The thinking is that during a confrontation, the shooter's flight-or-fight response will naturally result in a tightening of muscles, a restriction of hearing and vision, and an involuntary lowering of the body. Based on this, many believe that shooting positions should "embrace the inevitable."

The symptoms described above certainly do occur during many deadly force confrontations. But they do not affect every shooter in the same way and most often are adrenaline-flushed versions of that shooter's normal stance. Meaning, positions modify under duress but do not completely change. Defensive shooters who train to fire perfect shots typically will experience diminished capacity under severe duress, resulting in less-than-perfect shots. Is the shooter who trains only for "practical accuracy" not subject to the same diminishing effects of fear and adrenaline? It does no shooter any good to execute a weightlifting squat while trying to shoot a pistol. Forcing your large muscles (not accustomed to Olympic squatting) to tremble and shake while shooting is pointless, unschooled, and destructive. Reason this out for yourself.

QUESTIONS AND ANSWERS ABOUT BODY ALIGNMENT AND NATURAL POINT OF AIM

Q1: I lean back when I shoot and I shoot well. What's wrong with that?

A1: I have seen many shooters shoot accurately while leaning backward. There are two problems with leaning backward. The first is the magnification of recoil. Leaning backward or standing bolt upright can cause even a large shooter to rock back on his heels or even take a little step backward from light recoil (remember the Prove It exercise). When the shoulder carriage is slightly forward of the hips, the body will not be moved and the recoil will not be able to lift the shoulders. A second and related problem is balance. A shooter who leans back uses the handgun to counterbalance, whether he realizes it or not. When that shooter loses balance, which invariably happens, he will "pull" on the handgun, causing extremely high and low shots. Watch how the speed shooters handle recoil; it is always with a forward attitude.

Q2: My stance is different than the two you recommend and I am an excellent marksman. Why should I change?

A2: If you are an excellent marksman who manages recoil well, keep your shooting position. The proof is on the target and if what you do works, then let it be. However, if you cannot shoot to the standard given at the beginning of this book . . .

Q3: How hard is it to incorporate natural point of aim into my everyday shooting position? I can't be closing my eyes and shuffling around every time I shoot.

A3: When you train, always acquire your natural point of aim before firing. It will become your natural shooting position in relation to any target. Natural point of aim is all you have when the sights gets knocked off your weapon. Learn it.

Q4: Doesn't the tensing of muscles and an exaggerated forward stance enable the shooter to quickly force control of the firearm and drive the shooting process?

A4: There should be alertness to any stance, and the shooter should have a forward attitude. But that's not where the disagreement lies. If you were going to have brain surgery performed, would you seek out a surgeon who worked from a tense squat with an aggressive and exaggerated operating room stance? I doubt it. You would likely think, "That guy is a nut," and you would be right. A shooter does not need to play ninja warrior to fire a handgun.

Q5: Many competitive speed shooters fire with the head down, locked arms, and a tight, horizontal, overlap grip. How can you dispute what they do?

A5: I don't. This book is intended to lead a student to fire perfect shots. That will not happen every shot because humans make mistakes, but it *will* happen for the competent and dedicated student. Bull's-eye marksmanship, and its variations, requires the most accuracy of the handgun sports. Watch how unobtrusively those shooters fire. I understand the strong desire for practical skills and the natural distrust of traditional style training. However, *this book is an attempt to elevate foundational shooting skills through the only process proven successful, the Fundamentals of Marksmanship.* Learn to fire perfectly and then you can shoot at orange disks like your rear-end is on fire. *Everything else is a distraction until you are able to fire that perfect shot*—so please, don't use a head-down, locked-arm, tight-grip stance.

SUMMARY

Body alignment and natural point of aim are easy to learn, but they are contrary to how most of us were taught to shoot. Vigilance, self-criticism, and practice can make this the most natural of the fundamentals for the average shooter to consistently apply. Remember that aiming begins with the body and ends with the handgun. Likewise, extraneous movement begins with the body and corrupts the handgun. Sighting to fractions of an inch requires a still and stable platform. Reduce your negative influence by limiting muscular tension.

CHAPTER FIVE

BREATHING (LUNGS)

Choose the better shooting platform:
1. A smooth and level concrete walkway.
2. The bed of a pickup truck traveling on a gravel road.

If the reader believes there is a noticeable difference in the above two choices, you will understand the importance of controlling the lungs during firing. Disappointingly, breathing, once considered a serious subject in marksmanship discussions, is often dismissed as either insignificant or impractical. That sadly reflects the overall quality of current marksmanship education. I was recently told by an infantryman that the U.S. Army taught him to "breathe normally" during firing. There is worse advice; normal breathing prevents gasping from oxygen depletion. On the other hand, what if the soldier has just run half a mile with his equipment in 100-degree weather? "Normal" does not guarantee "stable." The actual problem encountered by breathing goes back to sighting—your eye must direct your hand to make adjustments within fractions of an inch. You cannot make such adjustments when your chest carriage is rising and dropping as if you are firing from the bed of a pickup truck, hurtling down a gravel road.

Prove It: Normal breathing is vertical movement

Your final Prove It exercise is also the easiest. Stand in front of a mirror while wearing no shirt. Breathe naturally. Watch the upper torso closely and you will observe the shoulders and chest rise and fall with each breath. Bring your hands out in front of you with your thumbs pointed upward. Allow the arms to rise and fall with the natural movement of the shoulders. Notice how far your thumbs travel with each breath and remember that sighting involves slivers of an inch.

You have proven that natural breathing causes dramatic vertical front sight movement.

Collegiate air rifle competitors wear heavy shooting jackets and gloves. These garments offered padded protection, but to whom—or what? Does the shooter need protection from the recoil of a glorified BB gun weighted down with a full wood stock? No; what those wonderful competitors are protecting *is* the air rifle. They are trying to prevent the influence of heartbeat and respiration on that rifle.

Breathing control is essential to minimizing movement for all shooters. The absence of oxygen causes involuntary trembling, muscle fatigue, light-headedness, diminished balance, and psychological stress, but breathing is movement. The marksman needs to minimize movement and maintain the breathing cycle. The solution is coordination rather than interruption. Properly coordinated, shooting and breathing can coexist indefinitely with no fatigue and perfect sighting.

NOSE OR MOUTH

We all know that we should breathe through the nose. That is why humans have noses. On the other hand, the mouth is designed to access the lungs when a greater supply of oxygen is needed. In marksmanship, we don't want to huff and puff, and yet there are instances when it is proper to breathe through the mouth. Shooters who are in poor fitness, overweight, suffer from sinusitis, or just have a cold will often benefit from breathing through the mouth. Firing after exertion or rapid heart acceleration will also require mouth breathing; therefore, every shooter should be familiar with it. The key is to not "over breathe" but only take in enough air to prevent the lungs from quick, shallow, jerky breathing that is disruptive to marksmanship. The reader will have to experiment with nose and mouth to determine which best meets his needs.

COORDINATION TECHNIQUE

There are different methods for controlling or coordinating breathing. Here is my preference:

1. Breathe normally.
2. As you acquire sighting (an ongoing process, remember) and begin your trigger press, pause your breathing in the middle of the exhale. Just press your lips shut, stop your breathing, and finish your trigger press.

The reason I prefer the half a lung full of air is because when the lungs are either completely empty or completely full, shaking will occur. Now you may be wondering if there is a practical difference between "coordinate breathing with firing" and "stop breathing until you fire." The difference in coordination is pausing the cycle without breaking it. Pause to fire and resume *that* exhale. When properly executed, this technique enables "normal" breathing with shooting. *A guideline for the length of a good breathing pause is about two seconds. If the shooter is delayed in gathering sighting or trigger press, he exhales and tries again. He does not hold his breath and keep trying to correct the error.*

QUESTIONS AND ANSWERS ABOUT BREATHING

Q1: How can I be sure that I am breathing properly?

A1: *If, upon firing a shot, you gasp, or even sigh, you are holding your breath too long.* If your shots string vertically, you are breathing while firing.

Q2: How can you shoot fast and use the above technique?

A2: The above is my recommendation for a best-case shooting scenario. You can also pause in the middle of the inhale. To fire very quickly, simply pause and fire multiple shots in about two seconds. Your goal is a stable platform; make your breathing work for you instead of against you.

Q3: Why not just breathe through rapid fire and acquire a hasty sight picture?

A3: Breathing while firing, particularly fast, multiple shots, will result in "zippering," a pattern of shots running between six and twelve o'clock. Speed is not an excuse to shoot poorly—pause your breathing.

BREATHING (LUNGS)

Q4: I can't fire my shot in two seconds. What should I do?

A4: When learning the Fundamentals of Marksmanship, it is not un-common to take a little longer to acquire sighting, get the other fundamentals under control, and achieve a good trigger press. If you need more time, release your trigger, breathe a couple of breaths, and try again. Don't just stop your breath, which you soon will discover causes all kind of movement problems. Keep the breathing pause within three seconds or so, and be patient as you acquire your skills. You will become faster as you prop-erly train.

SUMMARY

Proper marksmanship breathing never leaves the shooter sighing for a little more air. It allows for continued firing without physically diminishing the shooter through lack of oxygen. You have proven that breathing causes rising and falling of the upper body. Don't handicap your shooting by ignoring this simple discipline.

CHAPTER SIX

☆ ☆ ☆ ☆ ☆

PUTTING IT TOGETHER
(THE PERFECT PISTOL SHOT)

Many years ago in Baltimore, there lived a fellow named "Smiley." Smiley used to sell other people's property out of a garage near the harbor. A particular police officer took umbrage at Smiley's occupation and sent him to the hospital for three days. Upon his release, Smiley convalesced for a couple of weeks and then reopened shop out of the same garage. The officer, a proud member of Baltimore's Sons of Poland, was noted for combining respectable boxing skills with a whimsical tenacity. When the police officer discovered his earlier chastisement had failed to impress Smiley, he reissued it. Smiley, again, went into Johns Hopkins Hospital for three days. This time Smiley was laid up for a month. As soon as Smiley was able to get around, he went down to the same garage and engaged in popular commerce. A friend, shocked at this foolishness, grabbed Smiley by the lapels and shook his stitches loose. "You idiot! You took two bad beatings. If you don't get out of this neighborhood that cop is going to kill you. Why are you still doing business out of the same garage?"

Smiley shrugged, "It's not *my* fault . . . I just got good consistency."

CONSISTENCY

Consistency is the discipline that enables us to learn to shoot well. Consistency is also a part of the framework wherein we may shoot perfect shots. *Any serious study requires the ability to deliberately duplicate actions and control conditions.*

No one could learn to fly an airplane if the gauges and controls were continually altered. There would be no piano players if pianos did not share common keys representing the exact same notes on every piano. *The Fundamentals of Marksmanship can only be mastered within the practice of consistency.* A handgunner's shooting history is one of two things. It is either an unqualified mess of unrelated experiences that cannot be compared, measured, or understood in terms of skill evolution, or it is a ladder of measureable experience and developing skill upon which the shooter may climb to greater understanding and proficiency.

The following is an example of why consistency is important in everyday shooting. Bill goes to a friend's indoor range, where he is invited to shoot at a new reactive 50-yard target (big range). Bill usually only fires to 25 yards, and he doesn't recall how well he shoots at that particular distance. Sometimes he leans back and stretches his arms; other times, when shooting rapid fire, he leans forward and bends his arms. Bill likes to shoot all five of his handguns every range visit. He doesn't really remember which handgun was shot at what distance and where the rounds struck. Bill buys whatever ammunition is available for sale at the range. Bill is not a marksman, but he usually hits the target and sometimes does very well. Any shooter in Bill's situation would have the challenge of determining bullet drop and the magnification of error when firing at twice his usual distance, but Bill has no foundation to draw upon to make an informed adjustment. Bill is lost.

Here is the same situation with a different shooter. Frank is invited to the same big range, and like Bill, he doesn't usually shoot at 50 yards. Frank, however, systemically shoots at 3, 5, 10, 15, and 25 yards. He trains with one handgun per range session and always uses the same ammunition. Frank has perfected his stance and therefore keeps the same eye relief. He is a marksman and has been working on a consistent error that causes him to shoot 3 inches low left at 25 yards. Frank's 15-yard shooting is off about an inch, low left. At 10 yards, Frank's imperfection is even slighter and *almost* completely disappears at 5 yards. Frank does not always fire perfect shots, but he is a true marksman. He will determine that since his error is *exponentially increased* between 15 and 25 yards, bullet flight has succumbed to increased distance. Using his *exact* same stance, eye relief, and grip, Frank will forecast bullet drop and hold high right for approximately 10 inches and score a solid hit on his first 50-yard shot. That is the benefit of consistency.

Measure everything you do on the firing line. Know not only where your shots struck but why they struck at those exact points. When you *know* those things, you may adjust your sights (if necessary). When that is accomplished, you need change nothing else to shoot and learn. Be consistent or be lost. If you succeed with your feet 15 inches apart, don't change them. Be aware of what you do so that you may memorize and duplicate successful actions.

ON THE FIRING LINE

Let us assume that you understand and trust the Fundamentals of Marksmanship and are now ready to apply what you have learned. Here is your shooting process.

---

1. Command the field for safety. Know that your handgun and ammunition are suitable for the range on which you are firing. Be aware of human activity and your backstop. Make certain others know your intentions, and coordinate your actions with other participants. Organize your equipment, keeping necessaries on the firing line table or properly holstered. Keep other gear from under foot and off the firing line. Index.

2. Assume a natural point of aim toward your target. Aim first with the body and then with the hands. Check your body alignment using the closed-eye method. Get your feet on stable ground and hold your position.

3. Enter your shooting stance. As you assume your natural point of aim, begin acquiring your stance. Your shooting stance is not like underwear and therefore changed every day; your proven shooting stance is your stance for life. *Understand this—the stance that works for perfect shots at 3 yards is exactly the stance you will need to fire at 200 yards.* If you are not consistent in sight perspective (position) and eye relief (distance), you will not be effective in building skill. Natural bends in the joints do not disappear during rapid fire. The stance is your race car; don't switch out before the flag drops.

4. Grip and draw your weapon. Visually audit your grip at the beginning of every session. Confirm that you are as high as possible on the backstrap and your thumbs are off the weapon. Look for red bloodless fingertips (particularly on hot days or when fatigued). Load with the muzzle fully downrange. Cause the supporting arm to take the weight off the shooting arm. *Don't milk the weapon. If the grip is correct, leave it.*

5. Control your breathing. Whatever you have done prior to this point that may have elevated your respiration has passed. Allow your breathing to calm, and be aware of the rhythm. You may slightly part your lips and breathe through the mouth if necessary.

6. Acquire perfect sight alignment. Friend, this is it. This is the point where you will either master the pistol or the pistol will master you. All other shooter actions can be controlled through sighting, but if you cannot properly sight, none of this matters, and you would be better served learning to play tennis. *Be a fanatic! Study the tip of your front sight blade.* Notice every scratch, dent, ding, and discoloration. *When you focus to that degree, the spaces between the front sight blade and the walls of the rear sight will seem like twin Grand Canyons, and then you can pursue perfection.* Please, get that much from this book, and you will consider the cover price to be money well spent.

7. Acquire perfect sight picture. You learn where to hold through the experience of shooting perfectly at various distances. Know how to adjust your sights, how your sights are metered, and when to adjust them. Bullets drop over distance. Caliber, barrel length, and ammunition should inform your decision; know where your bullet will strike. *Pick an aiming point that appears no larger than the front sight. An exact aiming goal is required for exact bullet placement.* If you aim at a pie plate at 15 yards, you have to be imbecilic to expect a 1-inch group. Aim intelligently.

8. Press your trigger. Gather your slack; feel the resistance in the trigger. Ease it back, smooth and straight. *Your sights will judge your trigger press.* Feel the trigger, watch the front sight tip, and allow the pressure to build. Pressure moves the trigger rearward—it doesn't need to be "pulled."

9. Pause your breathing. As your trigger moves, pause your breath for the benefit of sighting. Press your lips closed and relax with lungs half filled with air. It will only take a second or two. This is the final effort to make the human conform to the stillness of the handgun. For a couple of seconds, everything is frozen. This is your window for a perfect shot.

10. Wait for the shot. Pressure the trigger while trying *not* to fire the weapon. Take up every available fraction of trigger travel with smooth, slightly increasing pressure. Keep the round in the firearm until you have cleaned out all trigger travel. Watch the front sight tip and maintain your perfect alignment and picture. Relax your shoulders and neck. When the trigger has traveled the distance required, the hammer will fall free. Generally, you won't realize the shot has been fired until after the bullet has reached its destination. The weapon will fire when it is ready; keep the pressure controlled, smooth, and constant. Enjoy perfect marksmanship for the second or two it takes for the hammer to drop. Children run through dark places; the mature walk slowly. Be patient.

11. Resume normal breathing. Exhale the rest of your air and continue breathing normally. If you arrive at this point through the preceding 10 steps, you will have intentionally fired a perfect shot.

Let's assume your attempt at firing the perfect pistol shot did not go well. What you need is some precise training, and a little perfect practice . . .

CHAPTER SEVEN

TRAINING AND CORRECTING
ERRORS (SELF-COACHING)

Whenever a child gets a new puppy, one of the first commands the puppy learns is "come." Children know that instruction depends on proximity and control, neither of which helps the self-educated. Any self-initiated enterprise requires some regimentation and self-discipline. There is a vast difference between "plinking" and practicing marksmanship. Shooting a handgun can always be fun, but now we will consider how to make it productive.

LIVE FIRE PRACTICE

At this point, the reader should understand the concepts and philosophy of the Fundamentals, if not yet the practical application. Live fire is continuing education, and it must be conducted in an organized and progressive manner.

SELECTING AN AIMING POINT

The aiming point (once again) must appear to be the size of the front sight tip or smaller. The best target I have found is made with blank paper and a black, thick-tipped magic marker. Turn a regular full-size target to the blank side and draw six crosses about the size of the human hand. Space them evenly. If you have been using paper plates as targets, for instance, you will discover an instant tightening of your groups (provided you are practicing proper marksmanship). As you fire at greater distances, make the crosses larger, but understand that the intersection of the cross never changes size, providing a very precise aiming point. By increasing the arms of the cross, you assist the eye in acquiring sight picture and determining the point of intersection. Another advantage in using crosses is economy—at least six targets for the price of one.

CHOOSING YOUR DISTANCE

The best way to learn how to shoot at 200 yards is practice shooting perfectly at 3 to 5 yards. Distance does not matter to a handgun. The handgun functions exactly the same when firing at any distance. The ammunition is another matter, subject to decreasing energy, the loss of speed, and the pull of gravity. The shooter will either adjust his sights or his point of aim to compensate for bullet drop, but he never has to compensate for the handgun. Whatever works at 3 yards works at 200 yards, as far as shooter and handgun are concerned. Using closer distances to establish your skills and do marksmanship maintenance is extremely practical. It is much easier to verify actual bullet impact, and there are no psychological distractions at close range. Wind can be a problem at greater distances, whereas a marksman working on fundamental skills will not have to separate wind and lighting problems from shooter error when working at close range. The only trouble close-range shooting may cause is in tempting the undisciplined eye to drift to the target. Rather than measuring and marking a group, the short-range shooter is looking for a single, slightly oblong hole. What could be easier?

WALK BACK

While short-range firing is best suited for developing foundational marksmanship skills, actual long-range shooting is necessary to discover points of aim for each distance and adjustments for wind. The absolute best method for developing long-distance skills quickly is the "walk back." The walk back depends on the shooter having mastered the Fundamentals of Marksmanship and being perfectly consistent on the firing line. In order to conduct a walk back, the shooter will need a brightly colored metal target (round or square are preferred), about 18 to 30 inches in diameter, and fixed at about torso height. Metal targets must be smooth to avoid backsplash, and the shooter must be cautious and clothed for possible ricochet. If no metal target is available, use a solid-color paper target of the same dimensions.

You will need an assistant to properly conduct a walk back. The assistant will serve as target spotter and therefore needs a pair of high-power binoculars. (I realize this is rather complicated for a range drill, but the rewards are incredible.)

Here is how the drill works. Keeping the spotter behind him and to the side, the shooter approaches the target within about 7 yards (3 yards with paper). The shooter draws his weapon, quickly acquires perfect sighting, and fires a perfect shot. This is not a speed drill; it is a rhythm drill, like dancing. As soon as the shot is fired, the weapon is made safe and the shooter walks back three paces and repeats the process. This continues to the shooter's internal rhythm. *Each firing occurs at about the same time at each distance. The consistency is what actually instructs the shooter.*

If you pivot to the right when you have finished your first shot, then pivot right after every shot on the walk back. If you kick dirt with the left toe when setting up your stance, do it every time. Don't invent superstitions for yourself, but *reproduce your actions at each distance in time with the rhythm you have created.* The spotter only speaks to inform the shooter of where the rounds are striking the target: "Six inches at seven o'clock," "edge of the target at six o'clock," and so on. The spotter does not give encouragement, analyze performance, or ask questions. The shooter says nothing; he just adjusts fire based on the spotter's reports. Shots will begin to drop and will go under the target if no adjustment is made.

Remember: the speed you establish during the first leg of the walk back will be the speed for every following leg. The pace should be deliberate, but no jogging, panting, etc. The shooter is walking away from the target, stopping every three steps, and firing. There is no physical exertion. Have your magazines or speed loaders ready. Make certain that reloading is not disruptive to the rhythm.

The walk back stops when the shooter misses. *Do not keep going after a miss—start over.* The walk back will teach you where to hold, reveal shooting imperfections by degrees, teach wind adjustment, and give confidence concerning your shooting limits.

HOW MANY ROUNDS?

One of the greatest offenses in marksmanship training is the use of too much ammunition during each string of fire. To fire perfect shots, you must train for perfect shots, and you cannot very well do that throwing half a box of ammo downrange at a whack. Each shot needs to be verified if anything is to be learned by the experience. Fire single rounds to begin every session, and work up to two-round drills. Two rounds lets traditional double-action pistol shooters train for the double-action first shot and subsequent single-action fire in addition to tracking every round. Three rounds is the maximum one should fire before verifying the target during marksmanship training.

The deliberation caused by one-, two-, and three-shot drills reeducates shooters and gives them a memory of only firing perfect rounds. In the introduction to this book, I mentioned the unfortunate incident that claimed the lives of California Highway Patrol officers, one of whom had been unintentionally trained to collect brass when emptying his revolver. Give yourself the subconscious memory of perfect shots. Waste nothing.

ROUTINE TUNE-UP

There are three exercises that should remain part of every marksman's routine maintenance: mirror check, natural point of aim check, and dry fire.

Mirror Check

In the days of the old barracks, it was common to find full-length mirrors attached to the walls stenciled with the instruction, "Check your salute." What we cannot see ourselves doing is apt to get sloppy. That certainly is the case with shooting stances. By using a mirror to check your stance, you will discover whether your "feel" is accurate. The errors you will be looking for are locked joints, leaning too far forward (which will transfer weight from the leading heel to the less stable leading toe), standing perfectly straight, leaning backward, lowered or cocked head, and feet too close (unstable) or too far apart (muscular tension and reduced mobility). Of course, you will have to first understand your subject before you can spot these errors.

Natural Point of Aim Exercise

You already know this one. Pick an aiming point appearing no larger than the size of your front sight. Put your handgun in storage safe condition. When you have perfect sight alignment and sight picture, shut your eyes for 5 or 10 seconds. Reopen your eyes and see whether your front sight has drifted right or left. Adjust your natural point of aim by shuffling your feet in order to move the body without twisting. If your front sight does not move to either side, you have found your natural point of aim. Do not be concerned with elevation (up and down), which is not a by-product of natural point of aim and is not naturally maintained even when the body is centered and relaxed.

Dry Fire

Deliberate dry fire of a handgun is marksmanship's own Prove It exercise. More may be learned quickly through proper dry fire then through the firing of a hundred rounds. There are few things as beneficial to the marksman as dry firing his centerfire handgun (some rimfire handguns may be damaged by dry fire; check with your manufacturer).

Dry firing is simply "firing" a weapon without ammunition. The weapon must be in storage safe condition and all ammunition removed from the practice area. *Dry firing does not preclude the four rules of safety.*

The reason we dry fire is to learn about our marksmanship skill more clearly than we could when contending with the disruption of recoil and the mechanical cycling of the pistol. Dry firing actually gives us a more pure look into our application of the Fundamentals of Marksmanship than we could otherwise hope to have. *At its core, dry fire is a sighting exercise and, as you know, sighting controls the other three Fundamentals. In fact, there is no better technique for improving trigger control than dry fire.*

There are two excellent dry fire techniques:

Common dry fire. Draw a small cross on your target at about head height. Place your target about 2 feet from the front of where your muzzle will be pointed. Using the four Fundamentals of Marksmanship, acquire perfect sight alignment and sight picture on the center of the cross. Press your trigger (single-action weapons will have to be cocked) while maintaining perfect sighting. Keep perfect sighting until you hear the "click" of the hammer striking home. You will witness the position and movement of the sights while experiencing the entire trigger travel. If your sights come off the center of the cross, you must release the trigger and correct. Watch the cross, press the trigger, and you will know whether you have perfect sighting and trigger control. When the hammer falls, wherever the front sight tip is pointing is where your shot would have gone.

Pencil drill. This is done similar to the above drill but will require the handgun to be much closer to the target. Insert a new and finely sharpened pencil (preferably a number 4) all the way into the barrel with the sharpened point sticking outward. When the hammer drops, the pencil will move forward an inch and strike the paper. A dot will appear below the cross. The goal is to dry fire several times making only a solitary dot.

Obviously, this is not going to work with a 9-inch-barreled handgun, but the average service weapon will work fine. It is a credit to pencil manufacturers that the pencils are true enough for this to work—I don't understand how, but it works. The point is, the dot is hard data, and either you will

 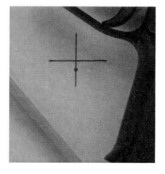

Pencil drill: pistol, target, and pencil.

Pencil drill aiming point (center of cross) and point of impact are not the same. The goal is one single pencil dot directly below the center of the cross.

Mechanics of the pencil drill. A new pencil is seated all the way into the barrel of a pistol in storage safe mode.

When the trigger is pressed and the hammer falls, the pencil moves ahead far enough to strike the target. (Note: An extremely sharp pencil is required.)

know that you have perfect sight (and trigger) control or you will know that you do not.

COMMON ERRORS OF THE BULL'S-EYE CLOCK

The bull's-eye clock is the generic black-and-white round target we all imagine when thinking about pistol targets, superimposed with a numerical clock face. A shooting error is any shot that does not strike at the center of the clock (the point of aim). This is applied to dry fire as well as live fire.

There is some dispute amongst instructors as to the interpretation of errors. The "voodoo" portion of an instructor's job is interpreting strikes on a target (that's why it's necessary to watch the shooter). When multiple shooting errors are committed, they may cover or even reverse themselves, making interpretation difficult.

The interpretations included below (which are for both right- and left-handed shooters) are based on what I have witnessed during years of firing line instruction. I do not recommend the reader be dogmatic about the clock system but rather be willing to test it. For simplicity sake, I have kept each error "on the hour," but truthfully, many of these errors occur between the hours and even overlap. So if you're hitting at three o'clock, take a look at the common errors between two o'clock and four o'clock. As with everything in marksmanship, thoughtfulness and patience is necessary.

BULL'S-EYE CLOCK OF SINGLE-SHOT ERRORS

Twelve o'clock
R/H, L/H Error (1): leaning backward
Solution: bring shoulder carriage slightly ahead of hips
Training: mirror

R/H, L/H Error (2): exaggerating recoil
Solution: shoulder carriage ahead of hips and natural break in arms
Training: mirror, dry fire

One o'clock
R/H Error: upright and twisted stance
Solution: body alignment, natural point of aim, and shoulder carriage forward
Training: natural point of aim exercise, mirror, dry fire

L/H Error (1): twisted body and exaggerating recoil
Solution: natural point of aim and shoulder carriage forward
Training: natural point of aim exercise, mirror, dry fire

L/H Error (2): leaning backward in the bladed stance
Solution: shoulder carriage forward
Training: mirror

Two o'clock
R/H Error: backward lean, hyperextended shooting arm thrusting wrist to outside
Solution: proper stance, natural break in the shooting arm
Training: mirror

L/H Error: trying to move back behind the sights (head going down, shooting arm coming up) while firing with an overgrip
Solution: proper stance and light grip
Training: mirror, natural point of aim exercise, dry fire

Three o'clock
R/H Error (1): hyperextended shooting arm that breaks the wrist to the outside
Solution: natural break in the shooting arm
Training: dry fire, mirror

R/H Error (2): perpendicular stance, which causes muscular tension toward the shooting side
Solution: body alignment and natural point of aim
Training: mirror, natural point of aim exercise

L/H Error: trigger finger leveraging off the thumbs
Solution: lift your thumbs
Training: dry fire

TRAINING AND CORRECTING ERRORS (SELF-COACHING)

Four o'clock
R/H Error: forward lean and hyperextended arms forcing shooting wrist to the outside
Solution: weight evenly dispersed on heels and balls of feet, shoulder carriage *slightly* ahead of hips, natural break in arms
Training: mirror, dry fire

L/H Error: overgrip
Solution: light grip, lift the thumbs
Training: dry fire

Five o'clock
R/H Error: twisted body alignment
Solution: body alignment and natural point of aim
Training: mirror, natural point of aim exercise

L/H Error: overgrip
Solution: light grip, lift the thumbs
Training: dry fire

Six o'clock
R/H, L/H Error: forward lean with loss of balance
Solution: proper stance
Training: mirror

Seven o'clock
R/H Error: overgrip
Solution: light grip, lift the thumbs
Training: dry fire

L/H Error: twisted body alignment
Solution: body alignment and natural point of aim
Training: mirror, natural point of aim exercise

Eight o'clock
R/H Error: overgrip
Solution: light grip, lift the thumbs
Training: dry fire

L/H Error: forward lean and hyperextended arms forcing shooting wrist to the outside
Solution: weight evenly dispersed on heels and balls of feet, shoulder carriage *slightly* ahead of hips, natural break in arms
Training: mirror, dry fire

Nine o'clock
R/H Error: trigger finger leveraging off of the thumbs
Solution: lift your thumbs
Training: dry fire

L/H Error (1): hyperextended shooting arm that breaks the wrist to the outside
Solution: natural break in the shooting arm
Training: dry fire, mirror

L/H Error (2): perpendicular stance, which causes muscular tension toward the shooting side
Solution: body alignment and natural point of aim
Training: mirror, natural point of aim exercise

Ten o'clock
R/H Error: trying to move back behind the sights (head going down, shooting arm coming up) while firing with an overgrip
Solution: proper stance and light grip
Training: mirror, natural point of aim exercise, dry fire

L/H Error: backward lean, hyperextended shooting arm thrusting wrist to outside

Solution: proper stance and natural break in the shooting arm
Training: mirror

Eleven o'clock
R/H Error (1): twisted body and exaggerating recoil
Solution: natural point of aim and shoulder carriage forward
Training: natural point of aim exercise, mirror, dry fire

R/H Error (2): leaning backward in the bladed stance
Solution: shoulder carriage forward
Training: mirror

L/H Error: upright and twisted stance
Solution: body alignment, natural point of aim, and shoulder carriage forward
Training: natural point of aim exercise, mirror, dry fire

FLINCHING

Flinching is not listed in the above errors, but it rates some explanation. Flinching is a shooter's anticipatory action to noise and recoil. Generally, when we say "flinch," we mean a physical shrinking back. In shooting, that causes high shots to the supporting side. However, most flinching is actually a pushing away to protect the shooter from recoil. *Most* flinched shots go low. The nature of flinching is to push the weapon as far away as possible and so the shooting arm is often hyperextended, though that is not always the case.

The use of dummy rounds (available at the gun store) randomly placed in a pistol magazine or revolver cylinder (revolver shooters can also simply not load all chambers) is the best tool for learning if you flinch. When the hammer drops and there is no recoil, flinching will be incredibly obvious. By repeatedly using dummy rounds, the shooter will not know *when* to flinch and will ultimately abandon that error.

LOOKING FOR THE BULLET HOLES

A shooter wants to look at the target, even before the round is fired. Of course, that means abandoning the front sight tip. Some shooters can be broken of wandering by holding perfect sighting for a three count after the shot is fired. That doesn't work for everyone. So, if we can't stop you from looking, we can at least make it not worth your while. On the cross target, you may take a black magic marker and make short slashes all around the impact area. The cross will still stand out, but you will not be able to distinguish a bullet hole from a black mark. After a while you'll stop trying. An alternative is to use newspaper with a lot of newsprint; this works fine beyond a few yards.

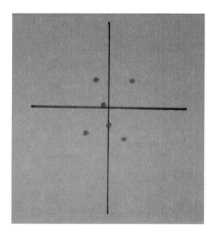

A target with six holes. The clarity of bullet holes in paper is a temptation for many shooters to shift focus to the target.

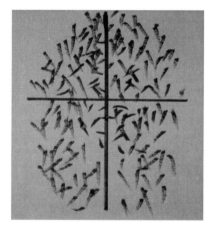

The same target camouflaged with slashes from a large felt-tip marker. Notice how the holes are less visible. (Note: When camouflaging, it may be necessary to darken the cross for visibility, as was done here.)

MULTIPLE SHOT ERRORS

"Chasing the Bull"—Shots surrounding the point of aim are the result of the eye leaving the front sight tip at the last instant and focusing on the target. The easiest solution is to follow through by staying on the front sight tip for a count of three after the round has fired.

Zippering—Shots that string between twelve o'clock and six o'clock during rapid fire are caused by breathing during fire. The solution is to control your breathing as explained in chapter 5.

Highs and Lows—Patterns of extreme high and low shots, which may appear in otherwise good groups, are the result of poor balance most often due to leaning backward. The solution is proper stance, which brings the shoulder carriage slightly ahead of the hips.

Strafing the Horizon—A horizontal shot group, particularly during rapid fire, is the result of twisted body alignment. The body seeking to return to a natural alignment pulls to the strong side during firing. The solution is natural point of aim.

"Starsky and Hutch"—When a shot appears at the top and to the supporting side of the target, the shooter is dramatically assisting recoil. The solution is to turn off the television and read this book. Dry firing would not be a waste of time either.

SUMMARY

A word or two about firing ranges. Please pick up your brass when finished shooting and clean your firing stations (regardless of what others do). Do not disrupt fellow shooters as you leave the firing line. We shooters ought to be among the most courteous people in society. Marksmanship is a responsibility for the conscientious and a sport for the civilized. Please look to your deportment at the range.

Analyze your shots and record your shooting. *If you don't know why you missed, you weren't watching your front sight tip.* If you were focusing like a proper fanatic, then begin to self-coach and cure your errors. Remember that every shot is the result of shooter action.

There is no mystery, nothing beyond the control of the thinking shooter—the marksman.

CHAPTER EIGHT

GUNS, GURUS, AND THE END
OF A REMARKABLY GOOD BOOK

GUNS

I have seen many shooters confound themselves with "handgun fever," i.e., trying to cure marksmanship woes with a better gun. So, I am somewhat obliged to mention firearm selection in a book on marksmanship.

The particular handgun just doesn't matter that much—I'm sorry but it's true. If you want to defend your home with a handgun, select a medium- or full-size handgun that fits your hand. It should be ambidextrous for a left-handed owner and be either a revolver or repeating pistol in .38/9mm up to .45 caliber, with a 3- to 6-inch barrel. The ammunition for your handgun should be a jacketed hollowpoint that travels somewhere between 900 and 1,500 feet per second. A little faster is fine if you are comfortable with it. A little slower is okay, too, if there is enough energy to expand the bullet. The bullets should be no smaller than about 90 grains and probably no greater than 300 grains. It doesn't really matter. Modern handguns made or imported into this country are pretty good today. Ammunition has so advanced that caliber is secondary. A big bore is better than a small bore with the same type ammo, but make certain you are comfortable with the recoil. If not, find the handgun/ammo combination that makes sense to you, in a handgun that is comfortable and affordable.

I was a firearms instructor for a police department that shared a range with the sheriff's office. The PD had Sig Sauer pistols and the SO had Ruger pistols. The deputies hated the Rugers. A typical comment was, "They're junk," but it was based on nothing. The Rugers were as reliable and as accurate as the Sigs. The real difference was—and I kid you not—the Sigs just looked cooler in Cop World.

When I was an instructor for a California sheriff's office, Glock came out with a .40-caliber pistol. Every idiot with a 9mm Glock had to have one. The marginal shooters became poor shooters, and some good shooters became mediocre. It was not the fault of the weapon. The point here is, whatever handgun you have is probably good enough, and the more time you spend developing your skill with that weapon, the better your handgun will perform. Remember, you have to know how to adjust for distance and weather, and you can't learn to do that as a member of the Gun-of-the-Month Club. (All things being equal, the most enjoyable of the lot is a nice .22 revolver. Sue me.)

Buy guns because you like them, not because you need them to be a better shooter. If you are absolutely certain that you need a different service-type handgun for improved accuracy, you had better be shooting at the limit of your current handgun's mechanical accuracy. Otherwise, how will you benefit from the margin of difference?

GUN MAGAZINES

I really enjoy gun magazines and keep them longer than financial records. My understanding of good shooting benefited through the writings of others, and my awareness of new firearms comes almost exclusively from monthly newsstand publications. That concludes my disclaimer.

There is more mischief worked on the shooting public by the sporting press than by second-world ammunition manufacturers. (At least bad ammo is sold cheaply.) Firearm appeal, like that of automobiles, is understandably subjective. However, evaluation of firearms and shooting techniques has lacked objectivity to the point where many novice shooters are firmly convinced that perpetual change in weapons and technique is necessary for competence. The truth is, we are in the age of reliable cars and reliable firearms. Some are better than others, but all major manufacturers make competitive guns. These narrower differences require greater exploration than "no mechanical malfunctions" after 50 rounds. Mechanical devices must be evaluated in objective terms, or the information given becomes pointless and even misleading.

This is a common failing among the gun press. Look through the next gun magazine you find that tests two hunting rifles in the same issue. There will usually be a stripped-down, no-frills, synthetic-stock rifle from an off-brand manufacturer and a beautiful custom or limited production job. If they shoot *exactly* the same, the ugly rifle will have "good, solid accuracy"; the beautiful rifle will possess "remarkable accuracy." It is worse with handguns because many writers can't shoot. If they could, they wouldn't try to pass off "center mass hits on a combat silhouette" as an evaluation of "usable accuracy." It is a disgrace, but very often gun writers will only test pistols with 4-inch barrels (duty length) at close range on large silhouettes using rapid fire. This is ostensibly done because (they claim) the weapon is designed for short-range defensive use and the testing should be a realistic measure of the handgun in its intended use. Any handgun must be accurate to be useable and safe. The ammunition does not stop traveling at 15 yards.

I once read where a law enforcement officer turned writer advocated carrying a particular handgun because he had always "felt" well armed while carrying that handgun. That is useless information and perhaps even misleading to an inexperienced gun buyer. Of course, writers should be able to give subjective opinions, but evaluations must be conducted by objective standards. Think while reading. Expose yourself to a greater variety of opinions when doing research on your next firearm.

GURUS

I am skeptical of anyone who names a gun-handling technique after himself. The "Weaver stance" attributed to Sheriff Jack Weaver was sufficiently different to merit others accrediting the innovator. I am not an adherent of that technique but recognize that it was an innovation useful in some circumstances, and today's shooters benefit from the influence of the Weaver stance on modern pistolcraft. However, taking a common draw technique, breaking it down into 12 laborious steps, and slapping your brand on it is disgraceful. I experienced that during a law enforcement course. The instructors had the students jerk through drawing their weapons in painfully small steps for nearly half an hour. Then the instructors told the students to execute all the steps in one fluid motion—not one shooter on that firing line could smoothly draw their handgun (including this imbecile).

Be cautious of who you allow to fiddle with your shooting. Choose instructors who have verifiably trained at least hundreds of shooters. That experience is necessary to read shooters and correct errors. Firearm instructors are instructors first; they shouldn't be foul mouthed, inconsiderate, or disorganized. Take no course that requires instructor worship or cult-speak to get through it (check with former students). Instructors don't have to be the best shots in the room, any more than a coach has to play better football than a quarterback. But the instructor must be a competent marksman and sufficiently so to have something to teach you. A last piece of advice: never take a course from an instructor who insists on wearing camouflage pants. Trust me.

Good shooting is like losing fat—we all know what we should do, but we'd prefer something a bit easier. Like diet plans, there is no shortage of gun magazine gurus willing to sell shortcuts. If you want to weigh less, eat less and exercise. If you want to be a better shot, learn the Fundamentals of Marksmanship, train critically, and practice.

Keep "expert advice" in proper context. Test everything before you accept it, including this book. Prove it or disprove it. Become a critic and discriminating consumer of shooting and gun information.

THE END OF A REMARKABLY GOOD BOOK

The Fundamentals of Marksmanship, once understood, require dedication to master. When you've established your foundational skills, seek out training in reloading, holstering, tactics, malfunction remedies, and the legal use of deadly force. There is always more to learn. Consider NRA membership to access their excellent programs.

If you have genuinely studied the information offered in this book, understood the Fundamentals of Marksmanship, applied knowledge to structured firing line experience, and corrected your errors, then you've probably discovered the truth . . . a rabbit out of a hat or a bull's-eye at a hundred yards—magic is magic.

ABOUT THE AUTHOR

Albert League, a former Marine Corps firearms instructor, has trained more than a thousand law enforcement, military, and security personnel. Following a stateside law enforcement career, he served as commander of an international police station in Kosovo. Recently, he has worked as a security contractor and firearm consultant.